ABOUT THE AUTHOR

Lyn, one of three children, was born in the city, raised in the bush, in Glen Innes and Baradine. Her father was in the Forestry Commission and her mother was a nurse. She was educated at St Ursula's, Kingsgrove, then graduated from Bathurst Teachers' College.

In 1971 Lyn met Brian the Publican at The Penshurst Hotel. Their first hotel together was the red-brick, suburban Union Hotel at North Sydney, followed by Sheila's—a unique, new entertainment concept, then McGettigan's, where an under-age disco brought together the teenagers of Sydney.

Tatts Tavern at Penrith was a tough pub. Never a dull moment, fondly remembered.

A tree change to The Lake Jindabyne Hotel, a huge entertainment venue showcasing Australian and International bands. Then her last hotel, The Kincumber on the Central Coast, where she was greeted by a warm caring community.

Lyn led a parallel life. After gaining her Hospitality qualifications at Ryde TAFE, 1985, and from Cornell University, she taught and trained Hospitality students throughout NSW, in clubs, pubs TAFE and UNSW. The slogan, "No More It's the Law" is the lasting result of one training session in Jindabyne.

She fulfilled a childhood dream when she graduated from UNE in 2001 with a BA in Archaeology (Aboriginal) and Palaeoanthropology and worked with the Indigenous mobs on the Central Coast.

Her three children, Danielle, Kate and Brian, lived and survived through this life and have followed her into Hospitality.

As she passed through the bar-room door for the last time, Lyn knew there were too many good stories to go untold.

She is divorced, writing, and enjoying life with her friends, family and grandchildren, and consulting in the Hospitality industry.

Behind the Bar-Room Door

TALES OF A PUBLICAN'S WIFE

LYN MCGETTIGAN

This is an IndieMosh book

brought to you by MoshPit Publishing
an imprint of Mosher's Business Support Pty Ltd

PO Box 147
Hazelbrook NSW 2779

indiemosh.com.au

Cataloguing-in-Publication entry is available from the National Library
of Australia: http://catalogue.nla.gov.au/

Title:	Behind the Bar-Room Door: Tales of a Publican's Wife
Author:	McGettigan, Lyn (1947–)
ISBNs:	978-1-925959-47-5 (paperback)
	978-1-925959-48-2 (ebook – epub)
	978-1-925959-49-9 (ebook – mobi)
Subjects:	BIOGRAPHY & AUTOBIOGRAPHY/Personal Memoirs; Entertainment & Performing Arts; HUMOR/General; HISTORY/General.

This work depicts actual events in the life of the author as truthfully as
recollection permits and/or can be verified by research. Occasionally,
dialogue consistent with the character or nature of the person speaking
has been supplemented. All persons within are actual individuals; there
are no composite characters. The names of some individuals have been
changed to respect their privacy.

Cover design and layout by Ally Mosher allymosher.com

Cover images from AdobeStock and iStock

For my mother and father:
Jack always had a good story and enjoyed a
drink while telling it,
Pearl often needed a brandy and patience to
listen to both of us.

Contents

PROLOGUE

Five p.m. Typical Friday night.

The wood-and-glass bar-room door continually pushes open. Smoke wafts out in a pungent cloud, mixed happily with the bar-snack smell of baby potatoes dripping with butter and liberally laced with salt, mixed with laughter, clinking glasses, conviviality and the inevitable:

"Another schooner of VB, luv."

"Gin and tonic, luv."

"How are you, Lyn?"

Greetings and waves of the hand before the punter gets back to the serious business of drinking and enjoying the company of mates.

"Here's the boss. Better behave yourself, Harry. She'll throw you out as quick as look at you."

The minute I walk through the bar-room door, I'm the woman of a thousand personalities: the psychologist, the sports whiz, the politician, the mediator, the crisis counsellor, the lawyer. I'm the one with the strong shoulders and willing ears, the woman who hears a thousand stories and meets a thousand characters, from the good through to the bad and the ugly. Behind this swinging door is a complete world. Bring a sleeping bag and you'll never have to leave. It's not half as interesting out there as it is in here.

This is my world and I love it.

Author's note—the following stories are told as I remember them. Some names have been changed to protect the innocent.

PART 1
THE PENSHURST HOTEL
1971–1977

My Life as a Publican's Wife—
How It All Began

The Penshurst. Nothing special about it. It was a typical suburban red-brick hotel on the corner of a street lined with shops on both sides, a bank, milk bars, Lawler's bedding shop, the post office, the fruito, the iconic fish and chip shop, and the TAB across the road. The hotel had a large tiled public bar in the middle, a lounge up the back and, somewhat away, a saloon bar, with an open beer garden on the side behind the hotel driveway. The beer garden was pretty basic: tables, chairs, plants if they happened to be there—nothing vaguely resembling today's fancy outdoor areas. The tables were rickety: made of slatted wood, liable to be wobbly because they were either old or the cement yard was uneven. The slatted chairs weren't terribly comfortable either. The driveway area was to be left vacant every Friday for Fred, the local millionaire, to park his Holden Statesman. Fred was a much-valued client, especially as he used to bring his employees from his nearby office and factory, ACE Gutters at Peakhurst.

It was a Friday afternoon in early March 1970, and the family had gathered at the Penshurst Hotel for my mother, Pearl's, 45th birthday—there was Jack (my father), Garry, Ian (my younger brothers, 19 and 21 years old) and me (I was 22). Naturally, the whole family had turned out to celebrate, as we all did love a drink.

By 6 p.m., we were all contentedly seated at one of the wooden tables near Fred's Holden. This was closest to the entry of the saloon bar and was a coveted spot by all the regulars. There was no breathalyser at that time, so no one worried much about driving to and from their local hotel.

By 7 p.m., we were well into the drinks, or shouts, as they were known. All of my family could tell a good story, especially Jack, and as the drinks flowed, the stories became more hilarious. This didn't take long, as Pearl drank brandy and dry, I drank whisky and soda, and the boys drank schooners!

Suddenly Jack said, "See that fellow there picking up glasses? That's the publican's son." He pointed to a tall, thin, dark-headed, good-looking guy.

"You're joking!" I replied. "Look at his bottom in those tight shorts. And look at those Bermuda socks!" He did not impress me at all.

As the evening progressed, the publican's son seemed to be around a lot, picking up glasses and chatting to the patrons, particularly the females, as he did so.

Ten p.m. came. By this time the publican's son seemed to concentrate on picking up the glasses around our table. He was very assiduously picking up glasses and clearing the table. Strange, but unremarkable. We continued to have a few drinks and tell a few more stories.

Suddenly, he loomed up again. "What would you like to

drink?" he said. We didn't hesitate to tell him—a Scotch and soda, a brandy and dry, and three schooners. Off he went to get them. After this shout had been repeated a few times, my father said to me, "I think he likes you. He'll probably ask you out."

"Don't be ridiculous," I said. "I don't know him. Anyway, I don't want to go out with him."

Sure enough, 11 p.m. came. By this time the publican's son had plunked four rounds down on our table in quick succession.

"Not a bad bloke," said my father.

"Good bloke," echoed my brothers. No comment from Pearl. No comment from me.

He was just doing for us what he had been doing for other patrons around us. Only in our case, a lot more regularly. The success of a pub depended on the personality of the pub owner and his family. Patrons expected to be shouted the occasional drink. Today, with hotels owned by companies, the shout by the publican is more often than not a thing of the past. So I thought nothing of it.

Then Jack said again, "I reckon he *is* going to ask you out."

I remained silent. But, sure enough, ten minutes later he paused in his glass gathering.

"Would you like to come out with me tomorrow night?"

"Thank you, but I'm already going out," I replied politely. Then, "Ouch!" I yelped. Jack had kicked me under the table! My two brothers looked at me in horror. I could see what was going through their minds—schooners lost.

Recovering quickly, I said, "What time were you thinking of going out?"

"Not until about 11.30," he replied. "I have to take some kegs and alcohol to a friend's place in Coogee. They are having an engagement party for a mate and his fiancée."

"That will be okay," I answered. "I'm going to the pictures in town and will be home about then."

Sigh of relief from the brothers.

On Saturday night, I duly arrived home from the pictures, escorted to the door—with my box of Dairy Milk chocolates under the arm (an expected gift of the time)—where I thanked and farewelled the guy who had taken me, and then went to get changed.

In no time at all, there was a knock on the front door. The publican's son, Brian, politely said hello to my parents who were dutifully waiting up to see that their daughter was being met respectably. The lateness of the hour didn't seem to bother them. In those days it was still normal to live at home until one got married. It was also common for a curfew, often midnight, to be put on the children of the house until they were about 21 years of age. Although I didn't have a steady boyfriend at the time, I had plenty of guys asking me out, and they knew by now I could handle myself. One was a Liberal party politician, one a racehorse enthusiast, one an artist, and the handsome one I went to school with (we used to call him the Coca-Cola Kid, because he worked at Coca-Cola). Adding another to the stable was no big deal—I had every night of the week covered! Besides, they knew him from the pub and he came across as, well—good-looking, good job, good Catholic—in other words, safe! I would be out much later than the midnight curfew normally imposed, so I suppose he fitted the mould of "safety" with a capital S.

Brian the Publican escorted me courteously to the hotel's green Holden station wagon, which was piled high with kegs and assorted cases of beer, wine and spirits, and a selection of glasses and ice. In the back seat sat his sister Margaret, who was all of 17 years! Margaret was still a pupil at Monte Sant' Angelo at North Sydney, a Catholic girls' school.

"I hope you don't mind," he said. "I had to bring her. She's keen on my friend's mate, Paddy, and he'll be at the party."

"Not at all," I politely replied, wondering what was going on. A chaperone, I thought—shades of Victorian England. I wonder what kind of party this is? Three kegs and assorted wines and spirits was a lot to take to a private party, especially as it didn't start until after midnight.

It all made sense when it turned out that the party was for a bunch of footballers, their mates and girlfriends. One of them was getting engaged. Everything in those days was celebrated with a party, and a party always featured grog. The usual venue was someone's backyard and this party was no different. So we went into the house with our valuable cargo; the kegs were taken to the backyard, the rest to the kitchen. The kitchen usually acted as the bar, and it was also a useful way to segregate the sexes—the girls stayed inside and the guys out the back talked "bloke's stuff" without interruption!

Party on! Brian the Publican remained outside, tapping kegs and dispensing schooners. I was in the kitchen drinking my

Scotch. Margaret was chatting up Paddy. Everyone was soon chatting to all and sundry as the spirits and bonhomie rose. All was right in the world, and at 6 a.m. it was time to go home. Everything was loaded back into the station wagon—empty kegs, stems, glasses, Margaret and Lyn.

"I'll pick you up tonight and we'll go to St. George Leagues Club for tea," said Brian as he dropped me to the front door. St. George Leagues was the big go in that area in those days.

"Okay," I said, and went inside to get some sleep before my mother started the 8 a.m. vacuuming. It was a ritual, and nothing stopped her, especially if you needed a sleep-in. Could start at 7.30 then.

Six p.m. Sunday arrived. Brian the Publican arrived this time in a more upmarket Statesman. Off we went to St. George Leagues. Conversation flowed. We talked about the footy results (St. George of course), the horse results at Randwick, the success of the engagement party. Then, the next significant thing:

"What is your name again?" asked Brian the Publican. "I'm sorry. I've forgotten."

The night went on, dinner, a few drinks, then, "I won't be able to take you out again for a while. I'm going on a Pacific Island cruise with my accountant, Kevin, on Tuesday. Would you like to come and see me off at Circular Quay? I've got some tickets. You can come on board and have a few champagnes before the ship sails."

This was the done thing. Guests came on board a couple of hours before sailing, and all drank as much as they could before the whistle blew to warn guests to leave the ship before it sailed. My friend Jenny and I took up his offer, and then stood on the Quay to wave goodbye.

"That's a funny thing, Lyn," said Jenny. "He's waving good-bye, but not to us. It's to those three girls up there."

"Maybe he's cross-eyed, Jenny, and we haven't noticed it," I said jokingly. "Don't forget he said that he will be back Thursday week, and is taking me out to dinner that night! I don't think there would be anyone else seeing him off."

We found out later that he wasn't cross-eyed and he was indeed waving to them!

Two weeks passed. Thursday night arrived. I was ready for the big date. I had been to Hurstville to get my hair done. This involved a wash and a set with rollers under the dryer. The trendy hairstyle was a pageboy with flipped up ends. Gradated Rollers were placed all over the head—large on the top to smaller at the ends. The dryer was a dome-shaped helmet that encased one's head. Hot air was blown onto the head. It was pretty loud when under the hood. Then teasing into the style and a can of hair spray to keep it in place. All in the name of vanity! Then home to get dressed to wait for the 6 p.m. knock on the door and the big date.

Seven p.m. came. No knock. Then at 7.30 p.m., my two brothers arrived home from the Penshurst Hotel.

"Well, Nett (as they called me), you can forget about going out. A stretch limo pulled up at the pub at 7 p.m. and the best-looking sort got out. She went in. She and Brian the Publican came out and got into the stretch."

They were right. When there was no sign of him, I should have forgotten about him all together, particularly after the incident of farewelling other girls as the ship sailed. Love is blind.

The next night he turned up at 7 p.m., bold as brass. Flowers, perfume and chocolates in hand.

"Come in," I said icily. "You are a night too late!" He started to try to talk his way out of it.

"You have made a mistake. It's tonight. I met this good-looking girl on the boat. She was Miss Queensland and the cruise was part of her prize. She said she had never been to Sydney before and asked me if I would show her around. I knew that we were going out tonight, so what could I do but show her around Sydney last night, especially after she had asked me up to First Class so often? I'm sorry, Lyn, that things got confused. Let's go now and I'll buy you a nice dinner at St. George Leagues Club."

I believed the story and forgave him—never even entered my head why he would be so often in First Class, leaving his friend decks below. Love is certainly blind. So we had dinner. Food tastes and venues at that time were certainly not sophisticated! To think he bought my favour with a Leagues Club dinner seems pretty funny now.

I went out with Brian the Publican for a few months. Time was drawing on and I was due to take up a teaching post in Sussex, England. I was to report at Honeypot Lane, the London head-quarters of the Education System, and soon had to have my inoculations and sail for England.

I said to him, "Brian, what are your intentions? I'm due to sail for England with my friend Carol in a few months. Are you going to marry me or not?"

"I want to marry you," he said.

"Okay," I replied. "I'll cancel the boat trip, ring Carol and tell her I'm getting engaged, and write to Honeypot Lane."

He then went to ask the permission of Jack, my father, who thought that he was quite acceptable, and suggested that we all go and have a few drinks to celebrate.

It was all very calm, I can't remember a great deal of excitement, but I guess there was, at least from my family.

We were married a few months later. Thus began my life as a publican's wife.

A Quick Honeymoon
Before Work Began

Our honeymoon was a South Pacific cruise on the *Himalaya*. This was eventful in itself. Just out of New Zealand we ran into a typhoon. Of the 1400 passengers, 1200 were seasick. I wasn't one of them; Brian was. He always attributes it to the guy who vomited over his thongs while we were balancing, slipping and sliding as the boat lurched, waiting for breakfast. A quick trip to the infirmary, a quick slip down of the daks, bared bottom, needle in and Brian was ready for bed. Once I saw that he was asleep, I went back upstairs. I thought that a quick port wine and brandy, the universal cure-all, was what I needed to prevent the same thing happening to me. I was right. I was fine, so continued upstairs to join in the day's entertainment, which was a card tournament—euchre.

"What are you doing here?" The woman was scandalised. This was 1971, and women were supposed to nurse their man.

"Why aren't you down with your husband?" Somehow word had gotten around the depleted passengers that Brian had succumbed to seasickness. He was a good-looking bloke, tall and dark-haired, and noticed by women.

"He's fine," I replied nonchalantly, bemused. "He's out to it and will be for about eight hours. I'll check on him every so often."

"That's not good enough." And she proceeded to tell me how she would organise a group of four women to take turns to make sure that he was all right. And this happened. Brian would later recount that every time he woke up there was a different woman standing over him. I can't recall how they got the key, but Brian certainly enjoyed the attention.

Our honeymoon had a few more interesting episodes, one of which was the euchre tournament.

Euchre was the popular card game and had many devotees. A certain level of skill was needed, but bluffing and luck played a large part. Brian was the master bluffer and had the luck of the Irish. We turned up the first morning at 10 a.m., ready and rearing to go. The tournament was like a round robin, which was held over three days from 10 a.m. until noon. The pair you were playing opposite was randomly chosen, and Brian and I managed to get through the first day, and turned up for the quarter-finals the following day. That there were so many people attests to the popularity of the game. We got through to the semi-finals. We got through to the finals. Our opponents were two hawk-like spinsters who made euchre their way of life. This pair played together at various clubs and tournaments and stayed victorious. The game started. Brian and I weren't a bad pair. I had been taught by my grandmother and didn't play the traditional way, but Brian was aware of my left-ball moves, all legal but "not the done thing amongst gentlemen". So the finals started. We won. The trophy, a small cup, was awarded to us, and all went away for what they thought would be a convivial drink. Not so.

"Excuse me, Brian," called the purser. High level, indeed.

"Yes, mate," answered Brian. "Would you like a beer?"

"No thank you, but that is not the reason I am here. I have received a complaint. The two ladies you beat in the finals of the contest have accused you of cheating."

"You're bloody kidding, mate. Those old chooks. What do you want me to do about it?"

"Would you agree to a rematch? With referees looking over the four players' shoulders and watching every play?"

"Not a problem," answered Brian. "Bring it on."

So the following morning we turned up to the auditorium for the game.

"Must be something on, Lynette. Look at the crowd! They've got the place wrong." At that moment, the purser turned up.

"I hope you don't mind, Brian. Most of the contestants from the tournament wanted to come and watch. You're a pretty popular bloke."

Thanks to all the drinks he's shouted, I thought uncharitably.

The card table was ready; the two ladies were sitting there, not a bit overwhelmed. We took our places. Four referees, looking a little self-conscious, stood behind the four players. Game on.

Deathly silence.

A huge cheer erupted after nearly an hour's play. We had won. It was probably symbolic that the last hand of the game had spades as the trump suit.

Drinks all round. Sherries for the two ladies.

Brian distinguished himself in other ways in Tahiti. We wanted to go deep-sea fishing. With visions of a huge fish catch we booked and the day came.

"Now understand," the crewman said, "once, we are out there, we don't turn back. If any of you are seasick, you have to live with it until we get back."

All heads nodded, including Brian's. It wasn't long before his head was nodding in a different way—over the side as he was violently ill. For some reason this usually male-dominated expedition was mainly female; Brian and two others the only males. The boys were in their element. Too many Tarzan movies in their youth gave them macho ideas. Then misfortune struck. Brian went from grinning king of the boat enthroned on the fishing chair to heaving, red-eyed, drooling semi-human wishing he could die and go to heaven. But all things end, and with the sympathy and kind ministrations of the females on board, he managed to make it to shore. Once on dry land, he returned to the generous, fun-loving male of reputation as he bought his fellow fisherpersons a few rums to settle their stomachs. No one had the heart to tell him that his stomach was the only unsettled one.

We continued on this Pacific escape. We stopped at Bora Bora, at Noumea, at islands where we swam, laughed and sampled the cocktails.

Then, a change of pace. We returned to our rented unit at Ocean Street, Penshurst and the start of hotel life.

A Learning Time

We started married life working in our chosen fields. While Brian continued to manage the Penshurst Hotel (where we'd first met), I was teaching at St. Ursula's College, Kingsgrove, where I had also gone to school. We continued like this for a year or so, not enough time to realise that Brian's work schedule would, in later years, nearly spell the end of our marriage. With both of us productive, I was oblivious to the loneliness that would overwhelm me when we started a family.

Brian was the worker in his family business, and this meant that he was up at 7 a.m. to have breakfast with his mother and father at the hotel before he was called to the cellar to take in the kegs. This completed, and with the bars restocked, he would shower and change and be back down to the bottle shop at 10 a.m., where he would work until his short lunch break. At about two o'clock, he would head upstairs for an hour's rest, and then go back down to the bottle shop until 8 p.m. Then he would head home. This routine didn't change. I would often call in and see him after school before heading home or out with fellow teachers for a drink or a game of golf. The fact is, if I didn't call in, I didn't see much of him. Saturdays followed the same routine as weekdays, and Sundays were always spent cleaning the beer lines and the cellar until midday. Often the afternoons were spent at a sporting match at a local park—usually involving the hotel side, especially cricket in summer, as this was good for business and for PR. All the alcohol would come from the hotel, so a good time was had by all.

I was introduced to the hotel game by Brian's mother, Jean. She was a publican of the old school and ran a tight ship. Nothing got past her. I already had a strong work ethic. I had started holiday work in a business that pasted pictures of a person's home on a calendar, for sale to the homeowner, when I was about 12, and then continued on to various pocket-money jobs until I started Teachers' College in 1964. Though I was no stranger to hard work, I did not fully understand the long hours and even harder work involved in the hotel business. Jean taught me well and kindly, and I remember her very fondly. She was a statuesque figure, about 173cm, with immaculately coiffed, thin, light-brown hair, thanks to a weekly hairdressing appointment. She had striking eyes. She missed nothing. But the thing that I remember most was the keyring on her belt. All the hotel keys were imprisoned there; she could be anywhere, anytime. And she was. She loved clothes, particularly in the colour blue, and shoes. Jewellery wasn't her go, and when, many years later, she lost her engagement ring, she replaced it with a fake diamond ring. Jean taught me everything she knew about the hotel business—including the tricks the staff got up to with their tills.

Bar staff were usually women, hence the term barmaid. Usefuls were generally males. Their job was to be useful to the barmaid by collecting, washing and reshelving glasses and ashtrays.

"If a barmaid or useful takes too many breaks, they could be going into the toilet to count their money. Watch if they leave the till open—they are not ringing up; they are putting the money in their pockets. Don't let them put coloured water in their tip glasses on the bar: you can't see what's in there. See if the coins in the till are in neat piles: they can count how much they have rung up and how much is theirs. Read your tapes. If too many 'No Sales' are rung up, they are stealing from you." And the gems of wisdom kept coming. But the most important thing, which later allowed Brian to wander, was the work ethic she enforced.

She also taught me the books. This was in 1970—before computers—and daily takings sheets, petty cash, and weekly and monthly reconciliations were kept by the publican's wife. The role of the publican was that of PR.

Kevin, Brian's father, largely filled the PR role at Penshurst. Kevin had a set daily routine, which Brian would later follow. Seven a.m. Mass at St. Declan's. He would arrive early and open the church with his own key. After Mass, breakfast, ferrying the daily takings to the bank, lunch, afternoon rest, PR drinks with a few customers, 6 p.m. dinner, the news on television, family rosary—"The family that prays together, stays together"—then Kevin went to bed about 8 p.m.

While some members of the family were praying hard upstairs, others were having boozy times downstairs. The breathalyser was being trialled at this time, as I was to find out. One Friday night, I turned up to the pub at midnight to have the local Sarge say to me, "Breathe into this, Lyn." I did. Most of the crystals turned green. We all had a laugh, another drink and I drove the one block home to the unit, as you did in those days. Brian's next meeting with Sarge (the local police sergeant) didn't turn out to be so laughable.

There was a charity event at the Mortdale Masonic Club which was in Victoria Avenue. In those days, everyone drank Resch's ("Resch's Refreshes" or "Resch's Wrecks"—depending on your outlook). Brian, blind drunk, had driven two cops home and this particular night he got home at 3 a.m. Typical bloke, he dropped his clothes on the floor and got into bed. The room started to move. He got up to go to the toilet and ran into a door. Then some scrabbling around.

"Are you all right?" I called.

"Yes."

"Big night, was it?"

"Yes."

Then he was back in bed again. The room started moving. Up again, straight into the same door. More scrabbling. He got up that morning to find out that the door he had run into was the wardrobe door. The room he was scrabbling in was the wardrobe. He thought I'd left the door open to teach him a lesson because he said that he would be home at 10 p.m. I didn't, you know. Upon reflection, it's a pity I didn't do it more often. It was an old freestanding wardrobe and, if it wasn't latched securely, it tended to swing open.

Rather than continue to rent, we decided to buy a house. We

looked at some in Penshurst, Oatley and Hurstville and finally settled on a red-brick one in Hillcrest Avenue, Penshurst. I had really liked one in Neirbo Avenue, Hurstville: a dark brick one that had lots of character. Hillcrest Avenue had none, but Brian's father was giving him a deposit so he had a big say in where we settled. There were reasons for this largesse, but suffice it to say that Brian's salary was $100 a week, thankfully supplemented by Jean's two roast chickens and a lemon meringue pie that arrived home with Brian at 1 p.m. every Sunday. This, in turn, was supplemented by my vegetable garden and lots of home cooking. It didn't do us any harm—it doesn't hurt to struggle when you are first married.

A couple of things stick in my mind, other than the birth of our daughter.

The buried treasure was one. You read about it, but you never find it. Jack and I did. The backyard at Hillcrest Avenue was one enormous rose garden planted by the old couple who had owned the house.

"Dad," I said. "Could you come over and help me dig up this rose garden? I'd rather have lawn."

Over he came one school holidays, and we set to work. We dug for three days and were down to the last quarter when Jack's shovel struck what we knew wasn't a root. He dug around it and unearthed an old Arnott's biscuit tin. We opened it. It was full of notes of various denominations. We looked at each other, scratched through it a bit. We both assumed the old couple had buried it and forgotten about it.

"Have you got their phone number?" asked Jack. "Ring them up."

I did. Great excitement at the other end.

"I'm coming straight over," said the old man.

Soon after that there was prolonged banging on the front door. Jack—dirty clothes, sweat-stained face—opened the door. The old fellow bounded in. No hello.

"God, you're an honest bloke, Jack. The missus and me forgot about that. Where is it?"

Jack produced the battered tin. The lid was prised off.

"Thank you." He managed to leave faster than any express train.

"Well, Dad, he won the lottery. I don't think we'll be so lucky." We weren't. We never saw him again, let alone a lottery ticket. They say honesty is its own reward?

We had a VB after the rose garden find, but quite a few more when "It Was Time". Gough Whitlam won the election on 2 December 1972. I was Labor, Brian was Liberal, so what to do except throw a party on election night where one of us and a few mates could drown our sorrows as the results came in? The other would celebrate. Our backyard by this time was a flat green expanse of buffalo lawn. Jack and I planted it courtesy of Oatley Park, where runners snaked everywhere and a few wet hessian bags full were definitely not missed. Jack had kindly built us a red-brick barbeque in the back right-hand corner. We were ready to party. The blokes were down drinking and cooking, and the party chef par excellence, Dennis Nowboy, was in the kitchen cooking up a storm in the Sunbeam frypan. Nothing could rival the taste sensation of cabanossi chunks fried up in Worcestershire sauce, not even the cheddar cheese cubes with red, green and white cocktail onions skewered onto toothpicks.

The election results came through, and for the first time in 23 years, Labor won. Naturally, the Labor supporters started a rowdy rendition of "It's Time". This infuriated the Liberals and a lively interchange followed.

"We'll fix them," I crowed. "Let's lock them out." Smart move. Lots of laughter. We locked them out all right. Suddenly Brian's hugely grinning face appeared at the sunroom window.

"Think you're smart, don't you? You can stay in there with the television for as long as you like. We've got the keg and the grog out here."

We looked at one another in dismay. They had played the trump card. All the grog was in the laundry tubs, beckoningly cool on ice. Sheepishly we unlocked the door. Treasure of one sort gone from that backyard was enough.

We lived there for three years until I was pregnant with our first daughter, Danielle. Life continued on as usual but with the addition of night classes in dressmaking at Summer Hill TAFE. Looking back, I sometimes wonder how I managed to make the children's clothes and some house furnishings. Needs must, I suppose, and with the help of my family.

However, we had saved hard throughout these three years and managed to move to a more family-oriented home at Merri Avenue, Peakhurst, and remained here for three years. We were very close to my parents and I remember, with gratitude, their saving of my sanity.

I have three children. The first, Danielle, was born on 7 January 1975, after I had spent three days on a stainless-steel table in the delivery room. Brian spent the time in the adjoining room with the nurses watching cricket. Every night I was wheeled back to the eight-person maternity ward until the morning when my first contractions started. The nurses ignored me—and the other seven mothers who were protesting on my behalf—until I had crawled across to the showers as instructed and promptly collapsed there. Then there was panic. I was rushed to the theatre where an emergency caesarean was performed. I will never forget my doctor, Joan Storey, urging the staff to hurry the preparation as she advanced with a scalpel. She was great. The staff were the problem. They approached me twice within two days to ask me not to tell the doctor what had happened. I didn't worry about the first incident—she would have known—the second was another matter. I did tell her that on the day after this operation; I was made to walk to the nursing room where I had to try to express milk. She had left strict instructions that the baby was to be brought to me. The number of adhesions she had to cut out with my second caesarean was, in some measure, testament to this.

"Hold your baby daughter," said the nurse to Brian as soon as Danielle was born. "She is struggling and may only live for a few more minutes." Brian must have been shocked and he remembers holding a little grey-faced child. But Danielle pulled through. About four years later, Danielle and I were watching a movie about an airline pilot who described his near-death experience.

"That's what happened to me, Mummy. I went down a long tunnel. There was a bright light at the end. I never got to the light. I had to turn back." She never mentioned this again, and when asked about it as an adult, she couldn't remember anything.

Life at Merri Avenue was not all beer and skittles. To me, rightly or wrongly, Brian appeared to be the worker, the one his family relied upon. Our relationship suffered with the long days, 7 a.m.–8 p.m., and the six-and-a-half-day weeks, but my loneliness caused by his long working hours worsened after the birth of our second child, Kate, in 1976. Emotionally, things got tough. It was hard to be alone for long hours with no adult company until late every night, and later still if there was a sports night or function he had to attend. Sure, I had my family, and they were marvellous— Mum would mind the kids while I did the weekly shopping, and I would call in there often, equally often bathing the children there—but ultimately I came home to an empty house to feed the kids and get them ready for bed. Brian, when he came home, would sit in a brown rocking chair and nurse Danielle to sleep before she was put into her cot at 8.30—and it was lucky that she was a night owl, otherwise he wouldn't have had much parenting time with her at all. It seems strange that Brian didn't insist that he come home earlier, now that he had a family. But he didn't. At times I tried to explain things to him, but those were the days of "grin and bear it"

Inevitably things got worse. I had taken to walking the girls around the block on a warm summer's night. This night I cried most of the way. It's funny how odd things stick in your mind sometimes. I was in the street walking past the school behind my house . I looked across at the house. My kitchen cupboards were painted a bright gloss yellow with green trim, quite the go at the time. I saw this bright yellow, glowing room. It didn't help that it looked warm and inviting. Subconsciously I made a decision. I had spent too many lonely days and nights, too much time crying, too long relying on the physical and mental support of my parents.

"Lyn has her own parents," Kevin told Jean, so she was limited in the support she could give.

There was a saying in Brian's family: "Kevin makes the bullets. Jean fires them." I was thoroughly miserable. I decided to leave Brian.

We were Catholic, so the obvious person to talk to was the parish priest who had married us, Father Phipps. Father was a wonderful, kindly man who had been a missionary in India for many years, and was still loath to wear shoes. It was morning, about ten o'clock, when I knocked on the presbytery door. He opened it. One look at his caring face and I burst into tears. He ushered me into the parlour, listened to my story, and then said, "You didn't marry Brian's family. You married Brian."

I have never forgotten his words. They came back to me many times over the years. I needed to remember them many times, too.

PART 2
THE UNION HOTEL

Back to School

The Union was our first hotel, but we were not to be alone as a family. Brian's Aunt Joan and her daughter, Donna, were to move in. Joan told us that they were there to "keep an eye on things". I always thought the reason was money—maybe Brian's family thought we would have wasted it; maybe they thought I might employ someone to help me with the children while I did the hotel work. There was a lot of "interaction" between other family members—who knows, maybe it was jealousy. Brian's father, Kevin, was prone to writing cheques for any reason. Maybe he thought Brian would pick up his bad habit. In this situation, things did not start off easily and would only get worse. With Brian's cousin Bernie, we were a permanent family of seven and Jean and Kevin (Brian's parents) were also there on a very regular basis. They had their own bedroom and sitting room always ready.

The art deco Union Hotel had been Tooth's Brewery showpiece and was a magnificent setting. The main staircase curving up to the living area was polished cedar, with a large, stained-glass bay window on the West Street side. The staircase led to a dining area on the right with a mahogany dining table for ten, and a matching sideboard. This beautifully proportioned room

29

was the site of many private functions involving police, brewery personnel, bankers and friends. Many were the times they would still be there at 5 p.m. before they were taken downstairs for their "cleansing ale". This was a tradition. Most functions anywhere ended with the group having their cleansing ale, usually a beer, before they went home.

To the left of the staircase was the living area. A long hall led past other bedrooms to the girls' room. This room was directly above the public bar and many nights I would check on them at 11 p.m. to find them bouncing on their pink rose-patterned bedspreads to the beat of *Blue Suede Shoes* and singing along with the lyrics. Barry Stanton, a rock legend, was a regular performer and as this was his closing number, they could parrot the words quite easily.

The large, green-carpeted bathroom was a feature and in the back, where Joan had her room, was another bathroom and stairs leading to the bars, with a sitting room opening onto the roof area. The linoleum-tiled kitchen with its two large pantries, which were sorely needed with so many residents, had another set of uncarpeted wooden stairs leading to the back bars. This hotel was typical in size but not in its beautiful decor. It could have been a happy home.

Our two girls, Danielle and Kate, loved playing on the rooftop area with their friends and their dog, Bussie, and pushing each other up and down the long hallway in cardboard boxes. The *Upstairs Downstairs* element played its part, with downstairs—the bar and its microcosm of life—being the fun part. Upstairs was for family, but still fun in its way.

Life followed its inevitable routine. Brian would be in the cellar at 7 a.m., then upstairs at 8 a.m. for breakfast with the family. Then Brian would go back down again, come upstairs to shower and change and open the bars by 10 a.m. Usually Joan got the money ready to be banked while I would make sandwiches for sale in the bars. The number of loaves varied from two on Mondays, to fifteen on Fridays. There were many varieties made: ham and salad, corned beef and pickle, chicken, roast beef. The list was endless. There were three half-sandwiches, Glad Wrapped, per pack and they sold for 80 cents. Before I had my third baby, young Brian, I would do these by myself, but two instances made me change this. I often think back to the time I so docilely made so many sandwiches and try to find an explanation—was it because a publican's wife was expected to work hard? Was it the Protestant work ethic, or was I just too stupid to know that I could change it?

I would start the sandwiches at 9 a.m. and finish as soon as I could. On Thursday and Friday this was not usually until midday.

I would hear two little voices: "Mummy, have you finished yet?"

I felt bad, but kept replying: "Mummy won't be long, darling."

I would reply on and off sometimes for two hours, while giving the girls a snack and drink. Eventually I employed a young girl, Michelle. She would come in and, except for Thursdays and Fridays, she would make the sandwiches. I would help the other two days, but only until 10 a.m. while the girls were watching their morning children's shows. After this, we would go to Balmoral Beach in summer for a swim and to St Leonards Park in winter.

There was freedom to run on grass and have a picnic. It was much better for all of us and gave me a welcome escape from the duties and dramas of our never-a-dull-moment pub life.

By 1981, all had settled down in the Union. One day I was in the Corner Bar, which was aptly named—it was on the corner of the Pacific Highway and West Street. This bar was the domain of the office worker, notably staff from the Australian Broadcasting Commission (ABC), whose office was next door in West Street; police from North Sydney station; the SP bookie and sundry others. It was a Thursday. This was police payday and they came for a drink and to get their pay cheques cashed. Brian would withdraw enough money from the bank to do this and then re-bank the next day. This was also "hot baby potato" day. It was a tradition with us that at 5.30 p.m. each day, bar snacks would be put on all bars. These were usually cheese and biscuits, but on Thursday, buttered baby potatoes, liberally sprinkled with salt, would be put out. The guys loved them, and the salt built up a bit of a thirst. It was one of these Thursdays that I put the potatoes on the bars, and decided to stay for a drink before going back upstairs to give the children their dinner. The children had been bathed by this time and the cook kept an eye on them as they watched television. I looked around. Brian was standing with a group of patrons, having a drink.

The time of the publican standing on the other side of the bar while the money goes into the till is over, I thought. There is no point in getting further teaching qualifications. I need to get hospitality training. I rang Ryde TAFE, went up and enrolled in the four-year, part-time course and started in February 1982. The Catering Supervisor's Course was the precursor of today's Diploma of Hospitality Management and included all subjects needed to successfully run a hotel, back and front of house. It was very thorough. I still consider it the best hospitality course of that time, and it had worldwide recognition as such.

The bane of my life was commercial cookery. I just couldn't seem to do anything right.

One day, as we were cooking our sauces, the chef said to me, "Leenette, Leenette, your sauce tomate, eet is shit. Eet is lumpy."

Then he passed on to my mate, Judy, whose background was as a home science teacher. We were great mates and used to stand together and have a bit of a chat as we were preparing the set dishes. Probably too much of a chat. Judy also set me straight on cooking skills.

"Ah Judee," he enthused, "your sauce tomate, eet is magnificent."

"Don't take any notice of him," Judy squeezed out of the side of her mouth. "There's nothing wrong with your sauce."

And so it went on. At the end of a semester, one of our exam menu items included cutlets. We were given a full menu and the time in which to cook and present it. After one such menu I heard from the front of the class as the chef cut and sampled.

"Ah Leenette, your cutlets, they are terrible," he lamented, then began to eat mine, rather than any of the ones presented by the 14 other students. Must have been all right—at the end of the class he was still standing.

"Don't think there's anything wrong with them," Judy whispered out of the side of her mouth, while trying not to laugh.

And so the cooking dramas went on. Came the day when we had to make custard from scratch. The custard was a shocker. I made the first lot. A dozen egg yolks used. I burnt it. Chef, with a disgusted look, allowed me to take the burnt saucepan out to the kitchen hand and try again. Total absolute disaster again.

"Ah Leenette, get the packet of custard powder." Disaster again. Mount Vesuvius erupted. "Take the saucepan to the kitchen. You scrub it."

Fair enough. But I had an ally in the kitchen I didn't know existed. He was a big, tall—at least 190cm—kind man of eastern European descent. He was very gentle and quiet, so I, and some of the other students, would often sneak him out something we had cooked. He looked at me, looked at the saucepan, and said, "I will do it."

"Thanks, but I will start. I can't go back in yet. Chef will know I didn't wash it." So I started scrubbing while chatting to him, and then he finished the saucepan. I went back into class, suitably chastened.

The last semester of year two, which was the end of our cheffing stint, each student took a turn as head chef, which entailed supervising and coordinating the meals for the restaurant. (Ryde TAFE had a restaurant as well as a canteen. Both were open to the public. For a cost of $20 in the restaurant, you could choose a three-course meal from the menu, including, I think, a beverage, alcoholic or non-alcoholic. The restaurant staff were students.)

All went swimmingly the day I was student head chef. The meals were cooked on time, ready to be plated when the orders from the restaurant came in. The teacher in charge of the dining room came to my supervising chef with a complaint.

"The wrong meals are being plated up."

I stood up for my team.

"No, Chef. We are plating up the right meals. The restaurant staff are taking the orders down wrong." Yes, right. He wasn't amused.

In spite of the cheffing dramas, I graduated in 1985 with two academic medals, 1984 and 1985. I was asked to go back and teach as soon as I had graduated as I had my Secondary teaching qualifications from Bathurst Teachers' College. Before starting teaching, I won the inaugural Carlton–Cornell University Scholarship (Carlton Brewery). This was in 1986, and there were three recipients Australia-wide, me and two guys. The scholarship was for a five-day seminar—"Financial Management and Planning for Profits"—held at the Hilton Hotel in Sydney, and, as Cornell was the premier hospitality school in the world, it was interesting, useful and informative. The following year, I attended "Marketing Management"—again presented by Cornell, in Brisbane. Also very worthwhile. In later years, the recipients went to America, to Cornell. The knowledge I gained through Ryde and these courses was invaluable to me throughout my 40-year hotel career. So, as well as the daily running of hotels and raising my family of three kids, I was set on the path to an academic career within the hospitality industry. Before I weigh in with more of the academic stuff, I must acknowledge that I couldn't have done it without the support of Brian. He looked after the kids the days and nights I was at TAFE.

He had a horrific first day of baby-minding. It was Kate's first day at school at St Mary's, North Sydney. Danielle was a model pupil. She was quiet and attentive, absorbing all. We didn't know that Kate had other ideas. Kate had two mates, Eric and Jack. The three of them would meet in the public bar at 10 a.m. for half an hour. Jack, with his schooner of Old, Kate with her pink lemonade and chips, Eric with his schooner of Resch's. Perched on their bar stools, they would solve the problems of the world. The subject of Kate's approaching school days must have come up.

"You don't need to go to school, Kate," counselled Eric. "Jack and I can teach you all you need to know." Music to Kate's ears. This idea lay dormant until Kate, uniform hanging, large schoolbag dragging on the ground, face as black as thunder, got to the first crossing, West Street into Ridge. Brian did have his hands full pushing young Brian in the stroller, half-dragging Kate along, the angelic Danielle trotting contently beside.

"I'm not going to school. Jack and Eric said they can teach me all I need to know." Immediately she sat down in the gutter. Brian somehow managed to get her up, pull her the remaining half-block, pushing Brian, then present her to Sister Ellen, the headmistress. No joy there. A swift kick to Sister Ellen's ankles and the two immovable forces met. Brian was not looking forward to going back to collect Kate at lunchtime. He needn't have feared. Sister Ellen had met worse than Kate in her life, but probably not many worse on the first day. A smiling Kate came out hand in hand with Sister Ellen. Her reluctant attitude to school didn't change but her friendship and respect for Sister Ellen has endured.

Then we found out what happened inside the classroom. The sweetest little pigtail-braided girl, Briony, saw her come in. Briony was playing with blocks in the corner. "Hello," she said, "come and play with me." Kate went over, looked down—the blocks were kicked over.

"I don't want to play," she said. Charming. Briony and Kate are still great friends. It beats me.

This hotel had many firsts. My first time as a mum with children at school, the first time I had met so many entertaining characters, and the first time I met a friendly ghost.

The Ghost of The Union Hotel

If ghosts can be called kindly and caring, our ghost was. But could this have been in restitution for her past? Our ghost was Mrs Veronica Monty, a famous thallium murderer of Sydney. Her victim was to have been Bobby Lulham. Bobby was an international rugby league winger for Australia, and also one of Balmain's brightest football stars in the '50s, a record try scorer for the club. Their story had all the juicy elements of newspaper headlines—sex, deceit, incest, prejudice, murder.

The story is this. Bobby Lulham, 26, and his wife Judith, 21 (Mrs Monty's daughter) were married in November 1951 and moved into their house in Ryde in June 1952. Mrs Monty, 45, had recently separated from her husband and had come to live with them. There was trouble early in the marriage between Judy and Bob, and Mrs Monty felt that he was not taking any interest in the house, but seemed to be taking interest in a girl called Gwen Stuart who was regularly seen close to him at football matches. Mrs Monty noticed this and took Bob to task over it. But maybe not in her daughter's interests. Mrs Monty and Bob started their own affair soon afterwards. One night, when Bob was listening to a cricket match, they had intercourse "in a moment of weakness".

According to Bob, it was initiated by Mrs Monty. He said she had "sexual power". The second occasion was on a Sunday morning when Judith was at church. The third was soon after on a day that Judith came home from work sick. For reasons known only to herself, it seems Mrs Monty decided to poison Bob. To divert suspicion from herself, she called the police and said that her husband had put thallium in the milk. On a second occasion she sent a letter to the police, composed of letters cut out of a newspaper.

Bob began to suffer the classic symptoms of thallium poisoning—tingling in the legs, loss of hair, stomach and chest pain. He went to hospital. It was after Judith and Mrs Monty visited him that Mrs Monty confessed to her daughter. What happened next is open to interpretation. Mrs Monty said that she "was down in the dumps" and was going to have a cup of Milo with some poison in it. Judith and Bob said they would have some as well. This fact got Mrs Monty acquitted. Bob said the poison in the cup could have been accidentally administered to him.

The Lulhams divorced. Mrs Monty committed suicide in a hotel room. She blew her brains out. That hotel room was at the Union Hotel. That room was where my baby slept!

When we bought the Union, Jim, who was the yardman, told us we had also inherited the ghost of Mrs Monty, though he didn't specify exactly where she was, thank heavens! All hotels in those days had their "yardman", so named because they kept the outside of the hotel clean by hosing and sweeping. They might also have a cellar man, who was often a drunk. Mrs Monty had been employed at the Union as a housemaid. Not long after we had moved in, her ghost made her presence felt.

At first, she walked up the long hallway around 11 p.m. every night. She would then walk into our bedroom, where I would hear her cross the room to the dressing table. She would lift every ornament off the table as if she was dusting and then put each one down again. She would then run a finger up and down the Venetian blinds then leave, walking back down the hallway. Although the first time we didn't know who the ghost was, the measured, leisurely tread gave the impression it was an elegant person. This would prove to be correct when we saw photos of her. And although she roamed the entire hotel, this was the only room she dusted. She only entered other rooms if she had a reason. She was given one soon enough by my father, Jack.

Jack laughed at the idea of a ghost. He didn't believe in them. But Mrs M got the last laugh! One night, Jack entered his room after downing a few schooners to find that the hot-water tap in the bedroom hand basin was running fast and furious. He pooh-poohed the idea that Mrs Monty may have done it, turned off the tap, and slept the peaceful sleep of the innocent. But Mrs M hadn't finished with him! At 11 p.m. he was woken by someone walking up the hallway. The footsteps passed his doorway. By the time he got up and got to the doorway, the footsteps were returning. They walked straight past him. He swore he heard them, but he saw no one. That was the night Jack the Unbeliever turned into Jack the Believer!

Mrs Monty became just another resident upstairs, as she rarely ventured downstairs. She didn't bother me. I spoke to her after the first dusting incident: "You can stay as long as nothing happens to the children." Nothing ever did, although the shadow of Mrs M could often be seen pacing the walls of the kitchen annexe. The cook was freaked out the first time, but also came to accept the "other" resident. The cook would tell the story of the shadow pacing back and forth, back and forth, settling only when the kids and I were sitting watching TV in the room in the next door.

Pearl, my mother, tells the story of the time she heard Mrs M calling out to our eldest daughter, who was seven at the time: "Danielle! Get Danielle!"

This was heard repeatedly a few times. Pearl was upstairs by herself; there was absolutely no one else there. Danielle was at her friend Clare's birthday party in St Leonard's Park, three blocks away. Pearl the Girl, grandmother extraordinaire, walked to the park, where all the kids were having a great time. Pearl's excuse for extracting Danielle has been lost in the mists of time, but extract her she did, and they walked home. As they got to the front door of the hotel, a freak hailstorm broke out. There had been no warning of this in the sky, nor did our ever-reliable weather bureau predict it.

This was not the only incident of Mrs M speaking out! Barbie the Barmaid and Gary the Cellarman were both spooked by Mrs M's antics. The first incident involved Barbie. I regularly took the two girls, Danielle and Kate, to Balmoral for a swim. We usually left about 9 a.m., before Barbie arrived for work at about 9.30 a.m. to set up the four bars. Setting up the bars in those days meant putting the bottles on the shelves and the runners on the bar. The bottles were locked in cupboards overnight to prevent theft; the runners were put on the bar to sop up any beer overflow from glasses, ashtrays strategically placed along them. (Bar runners were long towels, 65cm long by 30cm wide, usually with the logo of the product, such as "Bundaberg Rum" or "Victoria Bitter", on them. For this advertising, the company provided them for free, as they did the coasters that had to be set on every table.) The bar towels were taken upstairs nightly to be washed by the publican's wife.

This day, Barbie had collected the spare set of folded bar runners from upstairs and set them out on the bars. The kids and I came trailing back through the public bar, heading upstairs, around noon. Barbie saw us, screamed and went white.

"But you were upstairs!" she said. "When I went up to collect the bar towels, I called out to you! I said: 'Are you there, Lyn?' And you replied: 'Yes, I'm here.' I said, 'I'm just getting the bar towels,' and you replied: 'They're in the laundry.' I said 'Thanks,' and 'Bye.'"

"No, Barb," I replied. "It wasn't me. I've been out since 9 a.m. No one else is up there. It must have been Mrs Monty, the ghost."

"I'm never going up there again by myself," said Barbie.

I took the kids upstairs to bathe them. When we went into the bathroom, there was a lovely origami rose made out of white tissues in a small copper vase on the side of the bath. No one else had been upstairs while we had been away. No one else was home. Patty, the housemaid, was not working that day. The mystery remains. Believe it or not, but many people who worked

42

at the Union, from then to this present day, have had encounters with Mrs M.

Gary the cellarman had a much more extreme reaction when he encountered Mrs M. All of the older hotels have cellars under the premises, where kegs, and often other products, are stored. In the cellar of the Union, there was a room with slatted walls. This was the wine storage area and was always kept locked. On this particular day, a delivery of wine had come and Gary the cellarman was down there alone, putting it away.

"Are you there?" someone called out.

"Yes, I'm here," answered Gary.

"Are you there?"

"Yes, I'm here in the wine room."

"Are you there?'

"Yes, I'm bloody well in here," yelled Gary. By this time he had had it!

With that, the door slammed closed. Gary was locked in. Bear in mind that Gary had seen no one in the cellar. Although he had heard of the ghost and of Barbie's experience, he still laughed at the idea of a ghost. Gary was a down-to-earth Aussie bloke who only believed in what he could see and drink!

After an hour, Brian the Publican realised Gary was missing and went downstairs to see what had happened. When he found him, Gary was shaking like a leaf. For a guy with an olive complexion, he had turned a lighter shade of pale!

"Never again, mate. If I go down there again, someone comes with me!" said macho Gary. Mrs M had struck again!

Mrs M still "lives" at the Union and struck again in recent times so I heard. I was at a hen's afternoon at the Union about six years ago. One of the bar staff came up to me.

"I believe you used to live here," she said.

"Yes," I replied.

"Was there a ghost here?" she asked.

"Yes," I replied, "a Mrs Monty", and proceeded to tell the story. "Why?"

"Well," she said. "One night myself and another staff member were having a drink and playing a game of pool before we went home after work. Suddenly, a billiard cue picked itself up from the other end of the table and came hurtling at us as if it had been thrown. We've never stayed back since."

Mrs M probably thought they shouldn't be there after hours, or perhaps she was feeling lonely and didn't want to be left out! I told her that Mrs M liked company and now that the upstairs was empty and had no live-in family there—as Mike Willessee, the owner then, had converted the upstairs into offices and function areas—she may have come downstairs for company. Was Mrs M still living at the Union?

I forgot to mention that when the room young Brian slept in as a baby had been thoroughly cleaned after a fire, a semi-circle stain of blood came up on the newly cleaned carpet. Jim the yardman, who had been employed there when Mrs M was housemaid, verified that this was the room where she had committed suicide!

I should also mention that the kids had no accident of any kind while we lived there, even though they and their friends dangerously slid down the cedar staircase to the bottom level on regular occasions and engaged in pranks that I am still not aware of. It may seem strange that a ghost can care. I believe that only the good ones do and this must say something for Mrs Monty. Stranger still that you can talk to a ghost. There is a distinct advantage to this—Mrs M never answered back. Her actions truly spoke louder than her words.

The Goodies and Baddies Night

It was a night of contrasts at the Cross. Inside, in the Silver Spade Room of the Chevron Hotel, it was all warmth, glamour and abundance. Outside on the streets it was all pain, humiliation, degradation and exploitation. And this night brought both worlds together. It was called the Goodies and Baddies night, because the baddies (my nickname for them)—Sydney's more colourful characters—financed it in the name of charity, and Sydney's goodies—the police—were the guests, invited and paid for by the baddies. The colourful characters were Abe Saffron, George Freeman and Lennie McPherson. The goodies were the NSW Police Force, and two honorary "constables" sworn in for the night—me and Brian the Publican.

Weeks previously, the scene was the Corner Bar at the Union Hotel, North Sydney.

"Brian, would you and Lyn like to come to the big do George Freeman is putting on at the Chevron to raise funds for Odyssey House? It's a good cause. It's to help young kids with a drug problem," said one of our friendly boys in blue.

"Sure," said Brian the Publican, "it will be nice to see the boys again. They all used to drink with me at the Henson Park Hotel."

"We'll swear you in. You don't have to bring Lyn if you don't want to. There will be plenty of girls there."

The big night came. I went.

The police car arrived with a couple of the local constabulary, all dressed to the nines in suits and silk ties—very spiffy.

The Silver Spade Room at the Chevron was a magnificent sight—white linen tablecloths; sparkling silver and glassware; beautifully dressed guests. Immediately inside the doors were the girls lined up for selection for guys without a partner. These guys would choose the girl they wanted to "sit" with them for the night. The two police who arrived with us chose two young, attractive girls. The girls were so young! Remember, this was a charity function to benefit the drug-using young kids and prostitutes outside working the streets. To moralise: the cost of the function was more than paid for by the extra drug pushers on the streets that night, and the extra sales they generated.

As the night went on, things seemed to become a bit more lethal. George Freeman was obviously the king that night, and his wife, Georgina, the queen.

"One raffle ticket for $10, twelve for $100," said the seller who came to our table. The seller was an attractive young girl, but the persuader beside her was a brute. All the men at the table hurriedly put their hands in their pockets and came up with $100—one baleful look from the bruiser and this increased to a few more $100 notes given over. Meanwhile, big Normie Erskine, a celebrity of the time, thrashed out a number on the stage.

Suddenly, there was a hush. The raffle was due to be drawn.

The hand went in and the winning ticket was pulled out—"And first prize goes to Mrs. Georgina Freeman."

Amazing! The most worthy person won it, you might say. It was also noteworthy the first prize was two weeks on an exclusive tropical island off Fiji—which just happened to be owned by an ex-copper! The night wore on. The crowd got merrier. It was time for the guests to work the room, to renew old acquaintances.

I went up to the bar to get a dry martini. Standing there was a small bloke, smaller than me and I'm 153cm. I assumed he was a jockey. We were having a pleasant conversation until I asked him what he did for a living.

"I'm a cat burglar," he said as he quickly faded into the crowd. Of course, he was the right size for either burglary or horseriding!

As I went to the ladies, I passed Brian the Publican and four policemen talking animatedly in a corner. No doubt they were talking about the good old days when Brian's father was the publican at the Henson Park in Marrickville, the preferred pub for criminals. Suddenly, the group was surrounded by eight big men. The eight big men were not there to join in the conversation; their purpose was to enliven it. Just as it looked as if things might get ugly, George Freeman walked by, pointed to Brian the publican whom he remembered from the Henson Park days, and said, "That's my friend." The eight made a judicious choice. As though by magic, the eight disappeared into the crowd.

The story inside the ladies' toilet was not jovial. One of the pretty young girls who'd been lined up outside the entry door as we arrived was sobbing on her friend's shoulder. Her friend was consoling her as she said, "I don't like him. I don't want to be with him all night. He's mean and can turn vicious."

Her friend was reasoning with her. "You'll have to go with him. If you don't, you will be belted up. You'll be lucky if anyone looks at you afterwards." This little bit of reality was an undercurrent of the whole night.

Finally the night ended. As I got up to leave with Brian the Publican, one of the policemen said, "Why don't we go over the road and have a drink? I have a mate who has a share in the Penthouse Nightclub." The Penthouse Nightclub, with its own robot playing the grand piano, overlooked the eastern side of the Cross and was filled with colourful characters, most of whom had been at the Chevron.

Some say those were the days. All mates and all looking after each other!

Who Bashed Bernie?

Page 3, *Daily Mirror*, Friday, January 8, 1982. The headline read: AXE BURGLAR BASHES HOTELIER. Violent struggle in bedroom.

AN INTRUDER, wielding an axe and a knife, attacked a publican in his hotel bedroom today. The publican struggled with his attacker, who bashed him about the head and face. The publican, Mr Bernie McGettigan, 44, of the Union Hotel, Pacific Highway, North Sydney, was attacked when he challenged the intruder. Police said the armed man climbed into the hotel through a back window about 1 a.m. Mr McGettigan was asleep and heard the intruder in his bedroom. He struggled with the man, who bashed him about the head and face with a heavy object. As the intruder fled, he collided with Mr McGettigan's uncle, who was knocked down and kicked. Detectives have confiscated an axe, a knife and a brick. Police said the attacker could have bloodstains on his clothes. He is 180cm tall, 20 to 30 years old, with short brown hair. Detectives hope to interview Mr McGettigan at the Mater Hospital later today.

Bernie was a cousin of Brian the Publican. He had lived with the McGettigan family since he was 19 and came to Sydney to start work in the Public Service. When Brian and I moved to the Union Hotel in 1978, Bernie moved with us. He had lived with the family in the Royal Edward, the Albert Hotel, the Hensen Park and then the Penshurst, so it was natural that he would move to another family hotel. Our son, Brian, was born there in 1979 and Bernie was his godfather.

Bernie had been nicknamed "The Bustler" many years before because he was always "bustling" from one place to another, one job to another. He was a short man, 163cm tall, well covered, with a small beer stomach, and skinny arms and legs. He had his hair cut very short—very establishment. He was the typecast public servant: looked the part, never missed a day's work, rarely took a sick day, and was scrupulous in his work.

Why did this happen to Bernie, who was as they say "a man who would never hurt a fly"? And what really did happen? This is one story where you decide the likely scenario.

You have read the newspaper report. You will read accounts from Bernie, Jean, Pearl, the police and me before you need to decide.

Bernie's Story:

"I was working as usual on Thursday night. I counted the tills, locked up, and then took the money, which was in a calico bank bag, upstairs into my bedroom, where I would put it beside my pillow. Although the Union Hotel had a safe, Kevin, my uncle, liked to do it this way as it was what he had done every night for his 30-odd years as a publican. I respected his wishes.

"It was a hot night and the window was open. The door to my room was open. To get to my room you would have to walk up either the front or the back stairs to the first floor. My room was therefore in the middle of the upstairs corridor and there were bedrooms on either side. My cousin, Brian the Publican, his wife, Lyn, and the kids were away on holiday. The only bedroom occupied was one along from mine, but separated from it by a small conservatory and sitting room. My uncle Kevin and his wife, Jean, were sleeping in that bedroom.

"All doors leading from downstairs to up were locked. There was no one hiding anywhere downstairs. The hotel routine was that every night at closing, two staff members would go through the downstairs bars, toilets and bistro checking that there was no one hiding in them, locking up as they went. The doors to every bar were then locked. The bar complex in the Union was a bit like a submarine complex—the bars were compartmentalised and could be locked off from one another and from the three stairways leading to upstairs.

"Nevertheless, that night I had an uneasy feeling. I felt that there was someone in my room. I got up, turned on the light and looked around. There was no one in the room. I went to the toilet and then decided to go to the kitchen to look around. The kitchen was surrounded on two sides by a roof terrace. There did not appear to be anyone or anything unusual. I went back to bed.

"I was awoken at about 2 a.m. and there were shadowy figures standing in my room, although I am not sure to this day whether there was only one figure or if there were two. I think there may have been two, as I was hit by a brick and then attacked with a knife and axe. I slid down between the bed and the wall, trying to get away from them. I started calling for help. The last thing I remember that night was Kevin, the Publican's father, coming into the room. The next time I regained consciousness, I was in the Mater Hospital. Much later, two detectives from North Sydney Police Station interviewed me, and I remember telling them that I was attacked by one person. They told me that at the hotel I had told them that it was two people and they said that the first thing that you say is generally correct."

Jean's Story:

"My nephew, Bernard, was sleeping in the room just up the hallway from my husband, Kevin, and myself. Kevin and I were both over 60 years of age at the time. Kevin was the same build and height as Bernard, but I was taller and more solid. We had been in bed and asleep since approximately 9 p.m. when we were woken by Bernard calling for help. Kevin got up and went down the hallway to Bernard's room to see what was happening. Next minute, I heard Kevin calling out, 'Get away from him. Get away.' I put on my dressing gown and ran down the hallway. When I got to Bernard's room, Kevin was being pushed by two attackers. They had hit him over the head and there was blood on his hands where he had held his head.

"'Leave him alone, you cowards,' I yelled at them. 'He's an old man and he has a bad heart.' (Jean was feisty. Nothing scared her.) I advanced towards them, swinging my arms and calling out: 'Where is Bernard? What have you done to him, you cowards!'

Two figures pushed past me, almost knocking me over and I went to make sure that Kevin was all right and then I saw Bernard. He wasn't moving and he was covered in blood. Kevin ran up the hallway to the bedroom with the telephone and called the police. I didn't touch Bernard. He wasn't moving and I was afraid that he was dead. It seemed a long time, but soon the police came. I let them in and then waited with Bernard until he had been put into an ambulance.

"Thinking over the attack, I have come to two conclusions: The first is that the attacker was a German backpacker who had come to the hotel for a job. Without checking on her background, I employed her when the regular housemaid had gone back to New Zealand on holidays for a month. The backpacker had only been employed for two days when the attack happened, but she would have had time to see the layout of the hotel. She would know the entrances and exits. The two people had run down the hallway towards the kitchen. They had pushed a ladder up against the garden wall and gone down it and run into the car park. From there they would have run down West Street or to the Pacific Highway. The police found that a window had been forced in the kitchen."

The Police Story:

The police thought there must have been two attackers, even though later Bernard was not sure. "What we are told immediately after the incident is usually correct," they said. They were sure that the point of entry and exit was the kitchen and that when the hotel was closed that night, a ladder that had been in the garage had earlier been put alongside the hotel wall where it would not be noticed. Both assailants climbed the ladder onto the garden roof where they waited until all lights were out. They must have been there when Bernard went into the kitchen. After entering through the window, they would have left the door open for a quick exit. Kevin and Jean must have surprised them.

"However," they said, "there is another scenario. Bernard works as a Public Servant and could have unknowingly offended a member of the public. It would be easy for that person, or persons unknown, to have followed Bernard home by car one afternoon to see where he lived. Bernard kept a regular routine and worked a couple of nights a week to relieve his cousin. They could have very quickly ascertained his routine and then cased the place. The bashing with the use of unnecessary violence would support this theory. There was no attempt made to take the money, which would further support this theory."

Pearl's Story:

Pearl, my mother, was asked to come over the next day and clean up the blood as no one else was strong enough to do it. It was thought that because she had been a nurse, she would be the best person to do it. She said, "When I was cleaning up the blood, I saw the evidence of the violence of the attack and the route they took when they left the hotel. In Bernie's room there was a lot of blood and pieces of flesh with hair attached to it on the wall. There was a lot of blood on the wall and on the bed. All along the hallway there were fingerprints. I thought that one set was smaller than the other. I thought one set would have belonged to a man and one to a woman. I think it was the German housemaid, as she has never been seen again."

55

My theory:

I was away at Surfers Paradise on holidays with Brian and the children. We were woken in the early hours of the morning of 8 January. I remember the date as we had been out celebrating our daughter, Danielle's, seventh birthday at the Bavarian Steakhouse in Surfers Paradise's main shopping area on the night of the seventh. Brian the Publican left immediately for Sydney. We left for Sydney a week later, when everything was over. This was the early days of my life as a publican's wife, and was the first time that the family had been exposed to any violence and it made me more aware of security, particularly as the children were living in the hotel.

After hearing the facts, I believe that the attacker was the housemaid. I do not necessarily think she was a backpacker. I think she told Jean that story to get the job. She would have known that the regular housemaid was away and for how long, because if her partner had been around the bars seeing how to get to Bernie, he would have found that out. Hotels are a place where everyone knows everyone's business. The upstairs staff come down for a soft drink and always have a chat to the barmaid. The regulars listen and join in and find out all the facts.

The backpacker story that she wanted the job "for only a month" would have fitted in well. Jean had always been lucky with her staff, but she had always had staff with references or staff referred by a current staff member. Jean told me the story the girl had told her, and I think that the circumstances she used to get the job fitted in well with the short-term employment that Jean wanted.

Two years later, when Bernie was living privately, he was attacked on his way home from The Oaks hotel at Neutral Bay. Why? Was this related to the previous attack at the Union Hotel? Or was it random? We will never know.

Time Gentlemen, Please—
A Story of Armed Robbery

One of the hazards of pub life is armed robbery. The first one I was involved in happened at North Sydney one Monday morning. Monday was usually the day a robbery happened because the weekend's takings from Friday, Saturday and Sunday were always banked on the Monday morning. As these were the most profitable days, the takings were always good. Publicans usually took their money to the bank themselves on a Monday. The only precautions generally taken were that the publican left at a different time each day and by a different exit from the pub. Brian the Publican, however, was a creature of habit. He tended to leave around 11 a.m. and took the same route from the hotel to the car. He would walk through the public bar, as the car was garaged in the car park behind this bar. He always carried the same bag: a blue Grace Bros Travel bag. This day, nothing changed! He went through the public bar, a great area for crooks' observations (who would pay too much attention to a couple of blokes having a beer and a chat?), and would have followed his usual routine—go out through the side gate, open the roller door to the garage, get into the Holden station wagon, and head off for the bank. As he went through the bar he called out to me. "Hurry up Lyn. You'd talk on the way to your own funeral."

"Coming," I said. "Just having a word to Jack and Eric. See you later, guys. Look after the pub while I'm gone."

Jack and Eric were into their schooners of Resch's and Old, and into a good gossip. They were sitting on the same stools, at the same spot. Their cigarette smoke curled up from the ashtray in front of them. They nodded and they took another sip of their beer.

When I got outside there were two guys in front of the roller door. They looked like Laurel and Hardy. One was tall and skinny, and the other was short and fat. The tall, skinny one looked up, quickly finished pulling the roller door down, but didn't slide the bolt home. He started walking with a canvas bag. The canvas bag was long and skinny and was zipped closed. I remember noting this and realising there were guns inside and it would be difficult for him to get them out in a hurry.

"Hey! Where do you think you are going with that Grace Brothers bag?" I said. "Come straight over here and give it to me."

The fat one—in khaki overalls, white T-shirt and blue plaid overshirt, and a very bad black wig sticking out under his baseball cap—headed towards me. The skinny one—in khaki overalls, white T-shirt and red plaid overshirt—glanced over and then continued casually walking down the driveway carrying his long, thin canvas bag with him. The image of Laurel and Hardy still remains strong.

I forgot to mention that I was eight months pregnant and huge. On a short lady, the baby bump has nowhere to go except out. We couldn't get too close to each other. Laurel's beer gut matched my pregnant stomach!

"Listen, lady," he said calmly, with his beer gut very close to my pregnant bump, and the Grace Brothers bag clutched in his fat paw, "we have your husband under the car in the garage. My mate's in there with a double barrel shotgun, and if you try anything we'll blast your husband."

How stupid does he think I am? I asked myself. *Your mate would be a bloody idiot to remain inside a garage while his two pals walked away with the money.* I looked down, pretending to be scared, let him get about ten paces from me, and then turned and ran towards the public bar.

"She's running away. Quick!" With that, fatso ambled off with as much speed as he could muster, and I had reached the public bar.

There were four doors in the public bar. Three looked out onto the Pacific Highway and there was the one that led to the car park.

"We've just been robbed," I shouted. "Quick, you go to that door, Eric, and you, that one, Jack—go! Get the number plate of any car that moves." They shot up and out, but through the door that led to the other bar! In the space of a second, there were only two beers and two smoking cigarettes left standing on the bar.

Bloody useless, I thought and ran into the office to phone the police.

There are always the numbers of the police station, the fire station and the ambulance close to any phone in a bar. I picked up the phone and dialled North Sydney Police Station.

60

"Don't worry, Lyn. We're on our way," they responded.

Suddenly there was a very rapid, noisy movement behind me.

"Quick! Quick, phone the police! We've been robbed!" Brian the Publican had arrived in the office.

"I've done that," I said, as I proceeded to serve a customer a slab of beer. As usually happens, such as when the Melbourne Cup is due to run, or some earth-shattering moment occurs, a customer wants to be served! This instance was no different. As I rang up the money, a shooting pain went through my back, which at the time I disregarded. At the same time, the police raced through the bottle-shop door and proceeded to determine what had happened.

They were very helpful and while we were being questioned, two patrol cars were in the vicinity. Unfortunately nothing could be done as no one had seen the car they were in, or any car moving in any direction.

There were two lessons that I learned from this:

Lesson One: Don't disregard anything when you are pregnant. My son, Brian, was born one week later by caesarean. He was long and his limbs were as thin as spaghetti. The shock of the robbery had hardened the placenta and he hadn't been receiving any nourishment. He is now a strapping 183 cm ex-rugby player turned hotelier. The doctor was not impressed that I carried on regardless, as women do, when I casually told her what had happened two days later.

Lesson Two: Never worry too much about what the baddies are wearing. Look for distinguishing marks such as tattoos.

Maybe I am looking at life as it was back then, through rose-coloured glasses, when I think that crooks were crooks and only wanted money and beyond that they didn't use violence for the sake of violence.

However, hotel life is not all beer and skittles. As well as being hard work, there is always the danger that something violent may happen at any time and usually unexpectedly. The story of Bernie the Bustler is proof of that.

Squirt and the Sprocket Bar

The bar at the back of the Union Hotel at North Sydney was called the Sprocket Bar, named after the holes that are on the edge of a roll of film. It was a smallish bar, dimly lit, with alcoves and many separate tables. The barmaid was Billie. She was an institution: small in build, sporting an immaculate bouffant, tightly lacquered hairdo. She knew everyone's drink and, even better, she knew when they would walk in, and had their drink of choice ready. The characters who drank there were all working in the movies, in TV, or on radio. Some were freelance journalists. They were just terrific people—they loved the bar and they loved Billie. They would have their phone calls redirected there and would always rendezvous there with mates. It was their home away from home. When working, they would go away on shoots and often be away for six to eight weeks, or sometimes up to three months. While they were away, they had all their mail redirected to the Union. We were their private post office. When they were back in town, they would turn up again at the pub and it was nothing for them to put $1,000 or $2,000 over the bar for a drink for the mates. If they ran out they would just say "Keep it running. We'll fix you up tomorrow, Brian."

It was never a problem: they always did. Same if a cheque bounced. Never a problem. It was always fixed up.

I remember a character called Billy Grey, aka "China" (because, according to his mates, his eyes slanted a bit), who worked as a grip, and his dog, Squirt. Squirt was actually the higher-earning media member of the duo. Squirt was an intelligent, beautiful-looking, black-and-white cattle dog. He was a stunt dog in the movies and on television and he was good at his job. Squirt liked adults, tolerated children, and all in all was a gentle animal.

There would have been no Sprocket Bar without Squirt. There was no party without Squirt. He was one of the regulars. Each night he would trot in, lord of all, survey the crowd and head for his water bowl. Billie the barmaid always put it in the same spot at the end of the bar. Bit like the human regulars—they all had their spot! Once he had drunk his fill, or "downed his first drink" in human lingo, he would head for the table where Billy was, and lie down. If Billy was not there yet, he would head for the nearest table of his human mates and lie down. This routine didn't vary daily for as long as Billy and Squirt were working around Sydney. If, by this time, you are thinking that dogs are not allowed in bars, forget it! This was the late '70s and mates didn't dob on mates.

One day, Squirt didn't appear. It was well past his usual time. Most regulars are as "regular as clockwork". Squirt was no exception. Billy came in.

"Where's Squirt?" he was asked.

"I was a bit late finishing and he was too impatient to wait for me. He started off by himself. Isn't he here yet?"

Explanation given. Nobody thought any more of it and got on with the serious business of drinking and gossiping. After all, Squirt knew his way to the Union from any part of Sydney.

Billy and his mates waited.

The whole bar waited.

The whole bar waited anxiously.

Closing time at 10 p.m. was extended to midnight, then to 1 a.m., then to 2 a.m. Brian the Publican reluctantly called out, "Time please, gentleman." Patrons filed out, still a bit concerned but a few extra drinks had allayed some of the anxiety.

"Don't worry, mate," said Bill to enquirers. "He must have decided to go straight home. Had a long day, probably dog tired."

Brian the Publican wasn't too unfeeling a bloke though. He called Peter the Cleaner and asked him to come in early. "Mate," he said, "I know I'm asking you to put life and limb at risk, but would you leave the Sprocket Bar door open? One of our regulars didn't make it tonight and we are a bit worried about him. It's Squirt. If he turns up will you give Billy a call? Here's his number, and here's some coins for the pay phone."

The following day was a sad day. A sombre group of Sprocket Bar regulars turned up at 10 a.m., Billy included.

"Any news, mate?" asked Brian the Publican.

"Not good, mate," said Billy. "Squirt left Annandale where I was working, was happily pawing it across the Harbour Bridge to here, when he was hit by a motorist. I think we will all be here for a while, mate."

So started Squirt's wake. He was remembered in grand style.

Brian the Publican provided many free drinks to lubricate the never-ending stories of Squirt's exploits. Not to be outdone in turning a sad day into a reminiscing one, I got together with Joan, the bistro cook extraordinaire (she cooked Sunday lunches for the priests at St Mary's, so she had to be good) and turned on a super spread.

Squirt wasn't the only "stunt person" to be lost from the Sprocket family. Not that long after, a stuntman, Berry, so called because he always had a strawberry embroidered on his shirts, had a freak accident at a friend's home. He was leaning on the balcony railing when it gave way and he fell two storeys onto the concrete below. That was another sad day.

Vale Berry! Vale Squirt!

The Fire at The Union

Things were buzzing along as usual on a Friday afternoon in the Zodiac and Sprocket bars at the Union. Behind the scenes, things were also buzzing in the electrical box in the hall cupboard at the side of the entry to the Sprocket Bar and underneath the main cedar staircase leading to the upstairs living areas.

It was a normal Friday night—the hot salted-and-buttered baby potatoes were on all the bars. We usually brought them out at 6 p.m. for two reasons; to keep patrons drinking a little longer before going home, and to make them want to keep drinking anyhow—salt gives you a thirst! No thoughts in those days of food to keep patrons sober, which is the aim of food under the enlightened "Service of Alcohol" initiative. The patrons themselves were getting a glow—most of them had had a two-hour "settling in" period. These were happy times in the mixed crowd that drank there. Coppers and ABC staff were in the Corner Bar, forgetting their day and getting ready for the weekend. The Brothers football club, ably directed by Barry in between sips, and his mate, John, was in the public bar getting ready for their fundraising meat raffles, after which they were free to enjoy a few well-earned schooners. A mixture of radio personalities, "colourful" characters and the gay community was installed in the Zodiac, and the television and film guys were in the Sprocket, chatting and networking. Skinny the Penciller had just wandered in to set up the SP for the Harold Park Trots betting. In short, all were there: the usual crowd, the usual Friday night.

Meanwhile, upstairs, the family and I were also carrying on as usual. Mrs Monty, the ghost, had stopped pacing the room outside the kitchen and her shadow could no longer be seen on the wall. She knew the children were safe. The cook was cooking dinner; the kids were watching television: Pearl the Girl had bathed them and they were in their pyjamas. Little angels each one! I was having a wine; Pearl was having her brandy and soda.

Downstairs, Brian the Publican was happily serving, and loving the music the tills were making.

Cousin Bernie the Bustler was having a quiet few in the Corner Bar with Skinny the Penciller and Sid the SP before he came upstairs to have his dinner. Bernie, being a creature of habit, had his few and was upstairs by 6.30 p.m. Brian the Publican was having a few middies in between serving customers. The only person not having a drink was Jack (my father, and Brian the Publican's in-law). Jack was busily painting my son, Brian's, room. He was hanging for a schooner, but thought that he would finish first. Very wise for Jack. He loved a chat and once he got downstairs he knew he would be there for a while chatting and having a few schooners. He was a real character with a wicked sense of humour and myriad stories to tell. He never wanted for an audience and was loved by all.

Suddenly, one of the punters, Peter, in the Sprocket Bar, sniffed.

"I can smell smoke," he said. "It smells like plastic burning." No response. After an odd glance at him, all kept drinking.

"I can see black smoke," Peter said, quite loudly this time.

"Yeah, okay," his mates said. No one looked up. No one looked anywhere except to the bar, where Billie the barmaid, was alert to pour their next drink.

Suddenly, the strong smell of smoke was undeniable. Black clouds were billowing from the electrical cupboard. This cupboard was located near one of the exit doors, but exiting was not on anyone's mind at this time.

"I'll get Brian the Publican to call the fire brigade," said Terry, Peter's mate, as he nonchalantly lifted his schooner for another sip before heading to the Corner Bar.

Brian the Publican was a bit too smart to call the fire brigade. Why call the brigade, interrupt the patrons and the punters from their serious bets and drinks when he could solve the problem without interruption to anyone's Friday night, not to mention serious loss of revenue? He would simply douse it.

Only one or two curious patrons, one of whom was the alarmist, lifted their heads from contemplation of their drinks, or stopped their flow of interesting conversation. (In some corners, that interesting conversation had been repeated two or three times, but was nevertheless still interesting to their mate, who was lucky to have half-listened to it once, so intent was he on relaying his own interesting conversation. The magic of alcohol!)

Brian the Publican approached the cupboard with a bucket of water. He had opened the door and was about to swing the bucket when his friend Perko the Banker turned up. He took in what was happening and, being rather quick on the uptake, grabbed Brian's arm.

"Don't do that, mate," he yelled. "You'll electrocute yourself."

The drama was finally interesting enough for a small crowd to gather.

Thankfully a more aware patron had used the office phone to call the fire brigade.

The fire brigade arrived and quickly took control of the situation. "Everyone out," they called, and directed the patrons and punters to another exit. Desperately clutching their schooners as though they contained liquid gold (some holding a backup in the other hand for the drought they were anticipating), they reluctantly filed out. Only the affected bars exited, and then only as far as the Corner Bar. This bar, they considered, was safe as it was separated from the affected area by a solid door, a corridor and another bar. The coppers, the ABC staff and the public bar regulars drank on.

"Is there anyone upstairs?" asked the firey.

"The wife, kids, cook and mother-in-law," remembered Brian the Publican.

"Get them onto the street," shouted the firey. "This fire is directly under the main private entry door. Take them out a back way."

Perko sprinted up the stairs, followed by Brian the Publican.

"Quick!" they shouted to Pearl and me. "There's a fire downstairs. Grab the kids, get the cook on the way through the kitchen, and go down the back stairs to the Corner Bar. Join the group on the pavement outside the Corner Bar."

By this time, things had gotten a bit more desperate. The smoke was blacker, the fireys were blanketing the electrical box in foam. The crowd of onlookers had swelled. There was quite a sizeable neighbourhood crowd on the footpath. The Corner Bar was doing a roaring trade as some patrons were lucky enough to get an additional few schooners before the beer became warm and unpourable because the electrical current had been cut off. However, not all hope was abandoned. The beer in the fridges was still cold.

"Is everyone out from upstairs?" asked the firey.

"Yes," replied Brian the Publican.

So we all watched curiously as the smoke billowed out. Another five minutes passed. There was quite a party atmosphere.

"Oh my God! Jack's still up there painting," exclaimed my mother, Pearl.

Up went one of the fireys, who grabbed my father, Jack. Jack was serenely listening to 2CH, calmly working away in his paint-splattered shirt and trousers, but by this time desperately anxious for his well-deserved schooner. He was trying to get the last bit done. He could taste that schooner!

"I could have died up there," said Jack, as he safely reached the by now considerable crowd gathered. A loud cheer went up for Jack.

71

"Stop whingeing," said Pearl. "You're all right now!"

Rescue completed.

Pearl and Jack got the kids home to their house at Peakhurst while the rest of the crowd settled into Friday night as usual. But what a night! No electrical power: candlelight only. (All publicans at that time had a sizeable supply of candles due to the frequency of blackouts.) There was warm beer, then warm spirits, then warm wine as the refrigeration system lost its chill. The place was nearly drunk dry. Everything edible had been eaten—peanuts, Smith's Chips, and all the cold pies.

A warm glow of candles and comradeship flickered throughout the establishment. In fact, it lasted until 2 a.m. Doors securely locked, of course. Not to keep the patrons in, they were going nowhere, but to keep the police unaware. This was voted by the locals as one of the most memorable nights ever.

The Bomb in the Suitcase

It started off as an ordinary July night at the Union Hotel: drinkers drinking, punters punting, and blokes chatting up "sheilas". At this time of the night, the "sheilas" were lovely girls; as the night wore on each and every one of them would attain the level of supermodels. It is marvellous what a few drinks will do to the eye of the beholder.

The same phenomena were happening in every bar: Corner, Public, Zodiac, Sprocket. The media mob were in full force, all having a great time, albeit in different bars. The ABC—which was housed next door in West Street—were there in their usual spot in the Corner Bar; the TV and radio crowd were in the Sprocket Bar. We had Berry, China, Billy, Squirt, Rex and Peter and Geraldine, Graham, David, Michael and Chris.

Maggie, one of the regulars and a media person, had just met her bloke from Ireland. He had arrived a few hours before at Sydney Airport and cabbed it to the Union. On the way through to meet Maggie he asked Brian the Publican if he "might be leavin'" his suitcase in the office.

"To be sure you can," said Brian the Publican, his brogue slipping out. Begorrah, but the ancestors had left Ireland centuries before!

The Irish bloke was introduced around and everyone was soon having a good time—what else would you be doing with good company and good grog, as only the Irish and Australians can do? It came midnight and last drinks were called. Out wandered the patrons in a warm, comforting mood, aided by the company and the drink. Maggie and her mate left. They, too, were very warmly happy!

The pub was locked up. Staff and publican had their staffies— a few free drinks before they left for home. Brian the Publican went upstairs to his wife and kids.

Frantic pounding on the door woke us at 5 a.m.

"Mate! Mate! Wake up!' yelled Peter the Cleaner hysterically. "Get the wife and kids out! There's a bomb downstairs in the office!"

"Shit!" said Brian the Publican. Wife up, kids miraculously still asleep. "Stay here," he intoned heroically, "I'll go and see what it is all about." By this time, Bernie the Bustler was awake and trailed heroically downstairs, thoughtfully aided by Peter the Cleaner.

Peter by this time was white and hysterical and it was he who was clutching the half-awake Bernie.

"It's a bomb, mate," he wailed to Bernie, the whites of Peter's eyes showing.

"You'll set it off with your shaking, mate," said Bernie. "Calm down."

This conversation got them down the stairs and to the office door, where a loud ticking could be heard. The door was opened.

The ticking came from the Irishman's battered suitcase, airport luggage tag still in full view.

"Maggie's mate must be IRA," Brian the Publican astutely guessed. "I'll call the police." He proceeded to do so from the office phone, which was conveniently located next to the ticking suitcase. Bad luck if it had gone off and bad luck for the wife and kids. Our bedrooms were immediately above!

Brian the Publican dialled.

"Hello, North Sydney Police Station. Sergeant Earnest speaking."

"Mate, it's Brian from the Union. We've got a bomb here in a suitcase."

"Where is the suitcase and where are you?"

"It's right here beside me, mate, in the office. Mate, it seems to be ticking faster and louder."

"Where are Lyn and the kids?"

"They're upstairs."

"Get them and get the f—out of there. I'll call the Bomb Squad," he yelled. Brian grabbed Peter. Peter grabbed Brian. Bernie grabbed them both. No go—three bodies couldn't fit through a narrow doorway at the one time. Once the three of them got free of the doorway, Peter, Brian and Bernie hotfooted it to the street.

"Shit! I've forgotten Lyn and the kids," said Brian. "You two stay here and flag down the Bomb Squad." One wonders where else the Bomb Squad might have been going in North Sydney at that time of the morning.

Back through the street doorway went the intrepid Brian,

streaking past the ticking, murderous suitcase, falling up the narrow winding stairs and sprinting down the hallway. (He had been a top athlete in his day.) He came to a screaming halt outside the kids' doorways.

He ran in and grabbed two of the kids, security blanket, teddy bear and me (all in our dressing gowns) and yelled at the third kid to follow.

As our tribe got out onto the street, sirens were heard screaming up the Pacific Highway from North Sydney. The leading car jumped the median strip, screeched to a halt in front of the group and two blokes jumped out. A third struggled along with equipment. They didn't appreciate the small crowd of onlookers who had miraculously arrived, shivering either from fear, cold or excitement. Probably a mixture of all three!

We waited in anticipation. Thank goodness the bomb didn't go off. We were near enough to hear all that was going on, or be blown to smithereens.

Ten minutes later, we heard: "Strewth, Brian! It's only a bloody alarm clock. A big bugger at that."

In those days, anyone who went travelling carried his own alarm clock. Sensible people carried a version known as a travelling alarm clock. It was a small clock that had a lid and folded up. The Irish don't do things by half. An alarm clock is an alarm clock: the bedside one just bundled into the bag.

When Maggie and her mate, the bomb-carrying activist, were located, they had landed at Adelaide. Mascot (now Kingsford Smith Airport), the inside of the Union and Adelaide airport tarmac were the only lasting memories, indeed the only memories, the Irishman had of Australia. He didn't have a chance to see anything else. The Irishman was hauled off the plane by the Federal Police and sent back to Ireland. Some say he was IRA, who knows? His drinking mates swear he was only here for a good time and to see his girlfriend. It certainly appeared that way.

The Raid

An SP was a starting-price bookie, so named because he took bets from hotel patrons on race days. The SP bookies were all connected to a phone network, conveniently set up by some guys who legitimately worked for the PMG (Postmaster General's Office, as Australia Post was then known). One of the largest networks for laying off bets put on in the pub and for the latest odds was J&D, operating from a Sydney shire. The phone numbers of SP bookies were changed regularly, sometimes two or three times a week, and strangely enough, two of the PMG technicians drank at the Union. Many years later, one of them died tragically when he was set alight by hoodlums, and the other one spent a few years in jail. Good blokes really—just using the PMG van, and the PMG phones and phone lines, doing a public service for the punters of Australia.

So the SPs would give the odds of the horse that a patron was backing at the time at which he was backing it. It could have been 16–1, 20 minutes before the race, with the same horse only 8–1 at the starting time of the race. You collected whichever price was written on your card.

J&D was garnering the information from the track, but not in the usual way. No phones were allowed on the racecourse then, so a rather more laborious method was used. This operative rented a flat in a red-brick block of units on Alison Road, Randwick. One of the boys would be stationed at the window with binoculars. He would hone in on the prices displayed on the course bookies' boards and then this would be relayed to the "office". The pub SP would also phone to get the latest fluctuations. These large betting operatives served another function for the pub bookie. If a large bet was laid at the pub—and this did not have to be *too* big to be labelled huge—then the pub SP would "lay off" with the large betting operation, to cut losses. Laying off meant that any large bets the pub bookie took were telephoned to the large betting operator, who would accept them and agree to pay any winning dividends. It was an insurance policy in operation. The publican had to be "in the know" as this was the late '70s and there were no mobile phones. Depending on the complicity of the publican, either the office phone or the public phone was used.

But times were changing in the SP culture: Beck's Raiders had arrived. They were an elite, incorruptible police squad set up in Chatswood. Their task was to stop the illegal betting practice that was rife at this time so that the betting money could be channelled to the burgeoning TAB and then on to the government. They had wide-ranging powers. There were no holds barred. They could raid anytime, anywhere, under any circumstances and in any disguise.

The SPs were alerted to the arrival of Beck's Raiders by the public phone and the "cockatoo". The cockatoo was a bloke who stood on the corner of the pub on the lookout for cops. The cockatoo looked out for the 21 Division, which was the Consorting

Squad (criminals were not allowed to meet as they could be charged with "consorting" to plan a crime such as an armed robbery or even murder), or for police if it was a punting day. The term "cockatoo" originated from the behaviour of black cockatoos in the bush, one of which keeps watch to warn the flock of danger. So, when the cockatoo saw the 21 Division approaching in their Holden, he squawked and everyone disbanded. Likewise for punting. About every three months, someone had to be a fall guy. This was understood and accepted by both sides. The cops would take them away from the hotel to the station, or somewhere else away from the hotel, and charge them, and then they'd go to court and be fined $200.

The SP days were interesting. Everyone got looked after; everyone was part of it: people in government, criminals, footballers. A lot of those colourful characters are dead now— Georgie Freeman, Jimmy Goodman, Frank Osborne (also known as Ozzie the Barber), Jimmy Chute, Red Rider, Johnny Hart, and Reggie "Chow" Hayes. (Brian the Publican knew them from the Henson Park days.)

It was a normal Saturday afternoon at the Union Hotel. The Corner Bar and public bar were full of drinkers and punters, nearly all male. Racing forms were everywhere. The radio was blaring the races; TVs were tuned to the races. You could literally feel the excitement that was generated every time the blokes were together in this sort of boys' club. Every punter thought that he was going to win; the SP knew that he would win! In those days, every Saturday had a Melbourne Cup atmosphere. The cockatoo was in his place on the corner; the SP, Sid, was in his place leaning on the bar, having a schooner and shouting a few; Skinny the Penciller (by day the council garbo, and so named because he was pencil thin and kept that way by his rugged job) was sharpening his pencils; and Brian the Publican was serving behind the bar, and ready to get change for the SP when needed. Bernie the Bustler was bustling from bar to bar to check that all was in order before he took his place on the other side of the bar for a few schooners.

"They're racing!" Everything was travelling smoothly. About 3 p.m., two new punters arrived at the Corner Bar. One was a bloke in a wheelchair, who was also unfortunate enough to have his neck in a brace. The other, his mate, pushed him into a corner, got a couple of schooners, and they took out their racing guides. The mate took a casual stroll through the swing doors into the public bar.

"How do you get a bet on in this place?" he asked Barry the Footy coach, President of the Brothers Football Club and his mate John, both regulars. Barry could be distinguished by his uniform of stubbies and thongs.

"Just go to the corner of the bar, mate. See that skinny bloke chain-smoking? He's the bookie. He's got the form guide and a tally sheet in front of him."

"Thanks, mate."

The minder went over to Skinny, introduced himself, pointed out his mate, and placed the bets for them both.

This went on for a good hour. By this time, he and Skinny were like old mates. The next time the mate came over to place another bet, Skinny said, "Look, mate. You stay with your mate. I'll come over and take your bets."

"Thanks, mate." Skinny didn't see the gleam in the eye or the half-smile. The next race in Sydney was due to start. Over went Skinny.

"What do you want, mate?" said Skinny, pencil and ticket in hand.

Skinny got more than he expected, with $20 for an each-way bet that he put in his pocket with the rest of the payout money. The "unfortunate" disabled man suddenly sprang up from his wheelchair, ripping the neck brace from around his neck.

"You're copped, mate," he said.

Skinny went white. The healthy tan he had acquired on the garbage run faded.

"Shit!" was all he could get out.

Back at the bar, all evidence of punting miraculously disappeared. Quite a few punters, led by Barry the Footy coach, felt the call of nature and headed for the men's bathroom to flush their bets down the toilet. Sid the SP called for schooners all round. Brian the Publican innocently kept serving. The tally sheet disappeared.

"All right mate, come with us."

The unmarked car was on the corner outside the bar. Skinny was bundled in. Off they went, heading down the highway to North Sydney. As soon as the three were out of the bar and the car was safely heading down the highway, Sid the SP and Brian the Publican took up where Skinny had left off. Bernie the Bustler moved around the bars like greased lightning, serving the quickly recovering customers who wanted another schooner to soothe their nerves before they kept punting. First the winning punters had to be paid. They knew what they had won. They were honest blokes!

Meanwhile, Skinny was taken to the Victoria Cross, a pub that stood on the corner of the Five Ways at North Sydney, so called because the Pacific Highway and three other streets met at that junction. The police station was directly opposite the Victoria Cross, with the courthouse beside it. By this time, Skinny was in a panic. It didn't take a lot to panic him! He was ashen and shaking like a leaf.

"Why have you bought me here, mate?" asked Skinny, already envisioning himself doing a stretch.

"Listen, mate,' said one of the coppers, "just empty your pockets: just let everything in them fall to the floor, and then turn and walk away."

"I can't do that, mate," said Skinny. "I've got a lot of money in there and it's not mine. I have to take it back."

"Listen, mate, I'll say it again," said the copper. "Empty your pockets and walk away."

"I can't," wailed Skinny.

"Then, mate, we walk across the road. You're charged."

Two hours later, Skinny arrived back at the Union Hotel. He walked in a shattered man.

"What happened, Skinny?" asked the punters.

By this time, all the races had finished and all the punters were celebrating their wins or commiserating their losses with a few schooners.

"I've been charged," babbled Skinny hysterically. "I'll be in jail for the rest of my life. What will Gloria [his wife] do? What will the kids do? I'll never get another job. I'll be killed in there."

"Shut up, Skinny," said Brian the Publican, "and have a schooner."

"I need a bloody hundred," said Skinny, and started to swallow schooners as fast as Brian could pour them.

That evening, after the horse racing stopped and before the greyhounds at Wentworth Park began, there was a conference in the quieter back bar. Skinny, by this time, was crying into his beer. He sounded like a broken record.

"I'll never get out! They'll kill me in there. What is going to happen to Gloria and the kids?"

"Shut up, Skinny," Brian the Publican and Sid the SP said in unison. "Give us a bit of peace to work it out. When we find out when you are going to appear before the magistrate, we'll sort it out. We're all mates, so don't keep whingeing." That settled, the boys had another beer and poured Skinny out the door to go home and break the news to Gloria.

The court appearance date was two weeks later. Skinny had lost nearly a stone in weight over this time and had drunk at least two kegs dry. More than one street in North Sydney found a few of their bins had been missed on his garbo rounds. Skinny had his mind on other things, namely the kids, Gloria, jail. Brian and Sid didn't lose an hour's sleep. After all, those involved in the case were all mates, and didn't mates stick together?

"Skinny," said Brian the Publican, "I have word that the

magistrate is treating this as your first offence, which it is, you silly bugger. It's a wonder you haven't been copped a hundred times. All you have to do is appear, sit up, and shut up!"

The fateful day arrived. Skinny arrived at the pub just before ten am. He could hardly lift the calming schooner before he was due to set off down the hill to the courthouse. He got to the doorway of the hotel. He turned around. He fronted the bar again.

"Mate, I think I'd better have a double brandy. Give me a straw to drink it through. The way I am mate, I'll spill it on my safari suit. I can't afford to do that. Things are bad enough already!"

Cheered on by the regulars, including old Jack and his mate Eric from the public bar, Skinny finally set off down the hill, escorted by Sid the SP. Skinny was a picture of sartorial splendour: pale-blue safari suit; *Persil*-white shirt; subdued navy and pale-blue tie; white leather slip-on shoes. The image was spoilt a bit, as Skinny constantly pulled at the tie that appeared to be strangling him!

They arrived at North Sydney Magistrate's Court—greeted the coppers there, and all and sundry. Courtesies over, they sat down and waited until they were called. They waited. Nothing. Skinny was in a lather of sweat. A break was called. All retired to the Union, as had long been the custom, for lunch: Skinny, Sid, police, magistrate. Lunch was usually two hours.

The magistrate drank and ate his lunch in the Zodiac Bar. He knew Skinny and probably thought that he was having a quiet break from all pressures. How wrong he was! Skinny was drinking his schooner on the other side of the hotel in the Corner Bar.

Looking idly through the bar partition, alone with his nervous thoughts, he spied the magistrate.

"I'm going to shout him a beer and have one with him," Skinny told Brian the Publican.

"No, you're not," yelled Brian the Publican as he leant across the bar and grabbed Skinny's arm, "You can't be seen anywhere near him!" Skinny saw the wisdom of his words and had a few more schooners.

The magistrate, unaware of the danger from which he was saved, finished his lunch and started down the hill for the afternoon session. Once again escorted and supported by Sid the SP, Skinny staggered down the hill to hear his fate. One hour later, he was barely capable of standing, as the magistrate handed down his decision. Skinny may have been standing, but he was incapable of hearing the decision, so sure was he that he would be walking out the back door of the courthouse to the paddy wagon.

After a great deal of time and effort, Sid managed to half-walk, half-carry Skinny back up the hill to the pub. Skinny was beyond comprehending speech, so Sid didn't intrude on his thoughts. Skinny gratefully collapsed onto a stool in front of the bar.

"How did you go Skinny?" asked Brian the Publican, knowing that the sentence was a lecture and a $200 fine.

"I'm in jail. I'm in jail for two years, mate. What are Gloria and the kids going to do? What am I going to do? I'll be killed. How are you and Sid going to pay the $2000 fine?"

Brian the Publican and Sid the SP looked at each other and grinned. It was too good to stop the entertainment that Skinny provided. Being good blokes, they let Gloria and the kids know that Skinny was okay. Being equally good mates, they calmed his nerves to the point of oblivion.

Needless to say, things went on as usual that night. The $200 fine was probably paid with the proceeds of that night's punting. However, there were some changes in security. There were now two cockies: one to watch for any strangers approaching by car or on foot along the Pacific Highway; one to watch West Street.

One could say that Skinny's confidence was shattered, and that the lesson he learned made him more cautious. A month later, on a Saturday, my brother Garry and his mate Alan turned up to have a beer and a bet. They walked in. Garry was a solid bloke, Alan smaller with a moustache. They were greeted by Brian the Publican as old mates, and shouted a schooner in the Corner Bar. They walked into the public bar to study the Form. Skinny saw them, took in their appearance, and saw them take out their forms and settle in. Ten minutes later:

"Hey Brian," said Barry the Footy Coach, "where's Skinny?"

"Should be there, mate," Brian the Publican replied.

Skinny couldn't be found. Sid the SP filled in as penciller. Things went along merrily. It came time to settle up after the last race.

"I need some change, Brian," said Sid, handing over a wad of notes.

"No problem, mate. I'll get it out of the safe." The safe was a large walk-in located in the office behind the Corner Bar. Silence for a while. Then Mount Vesuvius erupted.

"Shit! What are you doing in there, you stupid bugger? You scared me half to death!" Brian staggered out of the safe, gasping. Smoke billowed from the safe. Skinny staggered out, cigarette still hanging from his mouth.

"Are they gone?"

"Who?"

"The police," Skinny rasped. "There were two of them in the public bar."

"You stupid bugger, Skinny, that was my brother-in-law and his mate!"

Easy Cruisin' on the SS *Thank You*

There was a good relationship between the police, the publicans, sporting bodies and SP bookies. Hotels sponsored many sporting bodies.

The Union sponsored the North Sydney police football team. The team would play every second Thursday at North Sydney Oval Number 2. It was a pretty rugged match. After the match, both teams would get down to the Corner Bar at about 4.30–5 p.m. to have a few drinks. My job was to bring down the food: hot dogs, steak sandwiches, and the ubiquitous hot salted spuds. After quite a few rounds, the police team would run a raffle to pay for their end-of-comp away trip.

The second year of the police competition, they decided that they would like to go to Club Med in Tahiti.

It was necessary to think of another way of raising the money for fares. Only so much could be raised from raffles, so another source of revenue had to be thought up. I don't know whose idea a harbour cruise was. All I knew was that the beer was to come from the Union, and that Skinny the Penciller and Sid the SP would be there to conduct some gambling. I think someone from the local football club had volunteered to man the on-board barbie. So on the night of the fundraising, I drove the hotel station wagon, loaded with alcohol, to a wharf at Kirribilli. *It was quite a good-looking boat,* I thought. It belonged to some other SP bookie, and he had kindly loaned it for the night. I was quite surprised to see so many patrons there.

How kind of them to come on a money-raising cruise, I thought. *Shows that there is a good relationship between police and public.*

When all the alcohol was unloaded in record time, which was itself not unusual.

"Have a nice night, boys," I said before I drove back to the hotel.

How naïve was I? I found out quite a few years later that supposedly there were a few strippers on board whose performances below deck to blaring music drew the attention of the water police. You guessed it! The party boat followed the water police to their headquarters at the Rocks, and then, it was rumoured, the water police, who were due to clock off, hopped on board to join in the fun.

There was enough money raised to send the full team and support staff of 18, with money left over. When the team got back, they told Brian the Publican it was the best trip they had ever had. In their words, "The French sheilas were very kind to them." At least, that was the interpretation that I was given! After believing in an innocent cruise, I suppose I innocently believed this too!

The Crisis

After young Brian's birth, I was warned to rest while in the hospital and when I got home. I tried. For the first two weeks, all went well. I would feed my three children, wash up, and when I put the baby down to rest, I would lie on my bed with the two girls beside me. Then, Brian Senior's parents arrived.

"What are you doing lying on your bed?" asked Jean at my bedroom door. "There's been a sandwich platter order and the girl in the kitchen needs help."

Stupidly, without a word, I went to the kitchen and stood there for an hour finishing the bar sandwiches and the platter order, then I crawled back up the long hallway to my bed. The three children thankfully were still asleep. The daily bar wash was also one of my jobs, but after this kitchen episode, Patty, who was the wife of Barry the football coach, came to help me as a housemaid. My two weeks of resting had really helped, but it was not easy living with so many people and before long things came to a sad and very nasty end.

One morning, as usual, Brian was down in the cellar. I don't recall why I wanted him to help me, but I went down to the cellar to ask him to come up.

"He's busy," said Kevin. "He's not coming up. Stay here, Brian," he continued, "you've got work to do."

With that, Kevin followed me upstairs. An angry tirade followed. I have no idea what was said or why. I stood immobile until Kevin's madly waving hands came closer. I won't go into the details of what happened upstairs but the next thing I remember is running down to the cellar, crying and in shock. I didn't have time to explain to Brian the Publican what had just taken place. It was the last straw.

"Brian, I'm leaving."

Kevin had followed me down.

"Let her go," he said. "You stay here, Brian." Brian looked at me, but didn't ask what was wrong or why. I went upstairs, hurriedly packed some clothes, got the children and we all piled into the VW Beetle.

Jean appeared at the window.

"Don't do this," she said. "If you leave you won't be coming back. Don't be a silly girl."

I didn't say anything. I couldn't say anything. She didn't understand the situation and was only trying, in her way, to mend things. I believed, erroneously then, that Kevin never wanted Brian to marry, but I never understood why. I thought perhaps that as a son, he was expected to stay single, to work and support his parents. Looking back, it was probably because Kevin knew that Brian had a "roving" eye. Nevertheless, things had come to a head that day in the most unfortunate way.

I had only one place to go—my parents' home in Peakhurst.

They were very surprised to see us, but quickly made us comfortable. We bathed and fed the girls and then put them to bed. Then dad gave me a large whisky and soda and I told them what had happened. The shock of it must have sunk in by this stage as I can't remember anything of the first night at Mum and Dad's. They must have been shocked themselves and wondering what would happen to our family. Divorce was not a common thing in 1978 and most mothers stuck it out for the sake of the children. I wasn't going to stick it out under the present circumstances, but I realised that my options were limited. I imagined that Brian would somehow pay for a unit for his family to live in—a house was not even contemplated. The kids were fine for the moment. They loved being with their grandparents and were having fun visiting.

We were there for two days when Brian arrived at my parents' home. We were easy to find: where else could I have been? I remember parts of this conversation. He asked me to come back, but I refused to return until his parents had gone. I told him what had happened. He wasn't aware of the main reason that I had left, but still, not supporting your wife is bad enough. He left. He came over three days later and told me his parents had left. They were going to live permanently at Surfers Paradise and would not visit again. Under these conditions I returned to the Union. A few months later, Joan decided to buy a hotel. She settled on the Clarence Hotel on Crystal Street, Petersham. She and Donna remained there until Donna married, then Joan sold and went to live with her daughter.

It was soon after this that Brian's father decided that he wanted to sell and buy a hotel in Queensland. He wanted Brian to run it. To his credit, Brian said no. This decision came at an opportune time. We had heard from our accountant, Kevin, that a bloke, John Crowe, wanted to open a new concept in North Sydney. Brian, Kevin and John started talking and soon the Jacobsens, Colin and Kevin, decided to be part of it. So, with this new deal in place, the family went their separate ways.

PART 3
SHEILA'S
1983–1990

The Magic That Was Sheila's

The start-up of Sheila's was an exciting time, as all new businesses are. Sheila's Tavern, 77 Berry Street, North Sydney, opened in 1983 and was largely the brainchild of an amazing ideas man, "Crowie"—John Crowe. It was the first of its kind and the prototype for many of the nightclubs and venues that were to spring up around Sydney like mushrooms after the rain. Optimistic Crowie went about setting up this new venue in his own characteristic way. Normally you would find someone who could run a venue before you started building it. Not Crowie. Crowie had most of his team—the architect, the builder, the showbiz gurus— but he needed THE someone to run it. He approached his accountant, Kevin, and outlined his ideas.

"Mate, do you know a good bloke to run this?" Kevin did— Brian the Publican! Brian was the ideal choice. He was larger than life, was a great PR person and he had a hardworking wife—me! Brian the Publican also had the advantage of being well known in North Sydney to bankers, advertising people, radio and TV personalities, footballers and police.

So with the stage set, a memorable meeting was convened in the dining room of the Union Hotel (after a few ales were had downstairs in the Corner Bar). In this amiable mood, all agreed to be part of this new concept and were prepared to give it a go.

John Crowe's nickname should have been "The Magician" or "The Dream Maker". Sheila's was John's embryo. He fed it, nurtured it, watched it grow and then gave birth to it. It was his baby and it became the fantasy of the '80s: the place where everyone wanted to be, where they could totally be themselves or invent a new persona.

Some people may have dismissed Sheila's as a pick-up joint. It was never envisaged as that, but if that was what happened, so be it. I think that a gentler, truer description would be "where girls meet boys and where boys meet girls" and, in particular, where a female out alone could feel safe. This was what Crowie envisaged.

Crowie had owned Grey's Bar in North Sydney. Grey's was a success, so much so that the publicans in North Sydney—Brian the Publican amongst them—complained so often to certain bodies, that it was closed down. To my knowledge, it was not closed for breach of licensing conditions! That didn't sit well with Crowie, and he determined to create something that would "blow them out of their minds"—a place so successful they would rue the day they crossed swords with The Crowe!

When Crowie decided he would have the most successful place in North Sydney, he set about doing just that. Before long he had found a great, empty, desolate space—a vacant floor above North Sydney Shopping World—a new complex in Berry Street, North Sydney. It was huge, with square metres of columns and cement.

Crowie's vision created two bars, an outdoor covered

conservatory, and a 13-bay bistro with a fully equipped kitchen complete with walk-in freezer, cool room and dry-goods store. There was a problem with the design of the kitchen area though: the architects wanted to put the cool room and the freezer outside the kitchen, next to the cellar. At this time I was still studying hotel management at Ryde TAFE and knew this was unworkable. The facilities had to be part of the kitchen. My reasoning fell on deaf ears—there was still a very strong boy's club operating!

If I can't beat them, I'll find someone who can, I thought. So I went over to Centrepoint where the Executive Chef at that time, Herbert Berger, was the top chef in Sydney. I had met Herbert when I wanted advice on aspects of my TAFE hospitality work and not totally understanding that he was probably the most respected chef in Australia, I had boldly fronted up and asked to speak to the Executive Chef. He had shown me over the complex he operated and explained the economics of running a large kitchen. I regarded Herbert as a mentor and friend, so I turned to him for advice with this problem.

"Don't worry, Lyn," he said, "I'll come over and speak to them." He did. The kitchen layout turned out exactly as it should have!

The two bars, one at either end of the tavern, were huge. As they had to be. It was normal that 600 people ate daily in the restaurant area and one thousand were served at the bars at night. On busy nights, there were eight operatives behind each bar. The architect, Peter Mulroney, and the builder, David Newman, did a great job bringing Crowie's dream to life.

The name Sheila's did not come about entirely by chance.

Crowie had everything in order, the space, the lease, but not the name. It came from a complete stranger, a lady who was sitting next to him on a plane.

"You seem rather quiet," said the woman. "You must have something on your mind." Crowie laughed. He was always laughing. He has a great, infectious laugh.

"I'm trying to think of a name for a place that I'm building in Sydney," he said.

"What type of place?" she asked.

Crowie described his plans in general, but said, "I want it to be a place where women can walk in, go to the bar, order a drink and feel secure and comfortable."

At this time, pubs were generally far from pleasant places to be in for a female. A woman could drink in any bar, but often the language was not good and the area was inevitably filled with cigarette smoke. Not to be forgotten was the silence that often descended when a woman walked into a public bar, or the many sets of male eyes that followed her.

"I don't want that kind of atmosphere," said Crowie. "I want the surroundings to feel comfortable and look attractive."

The woman thought for a while.

"Why don't you call it Sheila's?" she said. "If it's to be upmarket and female friendly, then that would give the right vibe. There is a magazine called *Sheila*," she continued, "why don't you get in touch with them? It could work well for both of you."

So Crowie did. The editor of Sheila magazine was Pamela Noon, and she and Crowie decided that some of their model photo shots could be enlarged and used on the walls. They were magnificent works of art and became part of the decor.

The next problem confronting Crowie was music for the venue, so he decided to enlist the help of the Jacobsens. Kevin Jacobsen was a well-known show business entrepreneur and at that time was bringing the biggest names in international show business to Australia through his company, Jacobsen Productions. There was also another string to the Jacobsen bow—Col Joye, much-loved entertainer and part of the Bandstand mob. They were like one big family. Jacobsen Productions could provide the entertainment and bring any big names who were visiting Sydney to the venue.

So, one Friday they all met in Jacobsen's offices. Some of the personalities present were Slim Dusty and Michael Edgley. Crowie described his vision and his dilemma—what type of music would be most suitable? The guys argued. Finally, one of them said to Crowie, "Look John, we could argue here all day and not come to a decision. We could charge you a fortune for a piece of paper that would mean nothing. So, we will leave it up to you."

With that, Crowie decided it was time for a beer and lunch. With further thought, he decided that '60s music would be the most appropriate. Crowie was miles ahead of his time in the Sydney music scene. He owned the Hopetoun Hotel in Surry Hills, which was the birthing place of many great bands. Crowie knew what he wanted so he set out to make Sheila's the music venue of Sydney. In actual fact, it was probably the music venue of Australia and many great bands and entertainers, such as The Cockroaches, the Angels, Enormous Horns, Generation, One Hit Wonders, Rockmelons, Hoodoo Gurus, Roxette, Paul Kelly, Digger Revell, Deni Hines, Debbie Kruger, Jacko, Oz Born Brothers, Kevin Borich, Bullamakanka, Redgum, Stormy Monday, Kamikaze Cats and many, many more, played there.

It also hosted stand-up comedy nights. One comedian I remember was Vince Sorrenti, who was just one of many. For the entertainers, Crowie built a fully set-up stage—lights, sound, curtains—with a mixer box and a DJ. There was a huge parquetry dance floor in front. It wore out within a month and had to be replaced with marble. This marble was too soft, so had to be replaced after a week by a team of workmen one frantic Sunday night with a harder marble. It lasted!

Facilities for the bands were not forgotten. There was a band room out the back furnished with lounges for their breaks and, of course, occasional tables for their "riders". A rider was a list of the drinks the band wanted (within reason), and these were supplied by the venue.

Beside the stage were two huge video screens, one on each side. Specially selected videos were played 24/7. These videos were made on a weekly basis especially for Sheila's, and were regularly rotated. Some of the songs I particularly remember were those of Annie Lennox and the Eurythmics, notably *Sweet Dreams (Are Made of This*), Robert Palmer, Boy George and Billy Joel. The sound and videos were managed by a super DJ called Brett, the in – house DJ, who cared about his sound, ambience and equipment like the true professional he was. Chris Kearns, who also DJed, enjoyed Sheila's as much as we enjoyed his DJ style.

Moreover, I thought that Brett was really kind and considerate. He knew I loved the song *December, 1963 (Oh, What a Night)*, sung by Frankie Valli and The Four Seasons, and he stopped whatever he was playing and put it on whenever I walked onto the premises.

"Do you remember Brett?" I asked my mate Bernice one day as we were reminiscing over old times and I was waxing lyrical about what great staff we had at Sheila's, and how they were always industriously doing their job whenever I walked in unexpectedly to check up.

"You know, he knew that I loved *Oh, What a Night* and always played it when I arrived. I thought that was really nice."

"Did you?" responded Bernice. "He played that to alert the staff that you were on the premises. You were pretty tough in your day."

"Oh!" was all I could reply as my mouth remained open.

When word of what they were doing got around the hotel industry, the general consensus of old-style publicans was that it would be a failure.

Crowie spoke to a radio announcer and described his concept, right down to the shocking pink baby grand piano and the chauvinistic coasters. More about these later.

"It won't work, mate," said the radio announcer to Crowie the day before the opening. "I've just surveyed a hundred people. Ninety-nine said they would never go near a place with a name like that."

This didn't worry Crowie. He came in laughing to tell the boys. It didn't worry them either—they were primed, confident eternal optimists, or else they hid their worries well!

"It won't work," repeated the hard-nosed publicans.

Crowie had the last laugh.

He was having a drink with his mate Colin Tidy, the well-known Sydney bookmaker, on opening night as they watched the place fill to overflowing capacity.

"Looks like it will be a success, John. The place is really firing."

"I'll let you in on a secret. This is how to get people in—free entertainment, free food, free grog!"

It wasn't necessary, but it was a brilliant opening stunt. Sheila's was the greatest Sydney success of that time. Opening night only presaged the amazing success it was to be!

Opening Night—A Blue Bruiser

Sheila's

cordially invites you to a

SPECTACULAR EXTRAVAGANZA

brought to you by the greatest entrepreneurs the world has ever seen. Under extreme duress and at great expense, this enterprising group will change this depressed society for you.

Opened by the greatest entrepreneurs of them all.
Witnessed by you on

Monday 30th May, 1983 at 7 p.m.

> Brian McGettigan
> Lyn McGettigan
> Col Joye
> Kevin Jacobsen
> John Crowe
> David Newman

77 Berry St, North Sydney

Opening night had arrived. The place was ready. The invitations had gone out—some declined (the local member for Bennelong, John Howard, being one)—the staff were all in place, the pink coasters were on the tables, and pink napkins and tablecloths were on dining room tables set for a total of 100 diners.

Chef Bob, who had broken his leg the day before (giving a new meaning to "break a leg") was in a wheelchair directing the cooking, starting with hors d'oeuvres for 500. The bar staff were behind the two enormous bars. The usefuls were on the floor—ten of them, ready to pick up glasses. Now—video screen on, and band in the band room—Brian the Publican, Crowie, Col Joye, Kevin and David were enjoying a beer before the 8 p.m. opening.

Not so me. I had been delegated the job of doorwoman along with Bob the Ladykiller and Paddy the Irish Street Fighter, who had fended for himself on the hard streets of Liverpool. An unlikely trio, but all formidable in our own right!

"How are you guys?" I asked as I approached the door in my red business suit and high heels. Appropriate dress!

"Have you looked outside, Lyn?" remarked Bob.

I looked outside. Sheila's had a curving ramp edged with palm trees that stretched from the front door to the street one floor below. The ramp was filled with people standing four abreast. I went to the windows flanking the top bar and looked again. The line continued 500 yards along Berry Street, then angled into Miller Street and out of sight.

"Looks like we'll have a good night," I said. "Don't forget the dress code."

We had a very strict dress code—for the guys: collared shirt, trousers (no jeans), and leather shoes (no runners). In those days girls always dressed up to go out, so no dress code for the girls. Brian the Publican's philosophy was that where the good sorts went, the guys would follow. He was right.

The doors opened. Some of the guests had the official pink invitation, others had the verbal "Brian invited us" invitation. No one was refused entry! We began cloaking coats and directed the patrons to the bottom bar and conservatory.

I stayed on the door until 10 p.m. and then thought it was time to join the party. The guys had the drift of the dress code and besides, the local priest, the brothers who had taught Brian the Publican, and the nuns who had taught our children were in there, in civvies. I thought maybe I should keep an eye on them and make sure that they were okay.

The party was in full swing, as all parties are when the grog and food are free. However, as things go, there is always a greedy group. They had stationed themselves in the prime position—at the end of the bottom bar and in front of the kitchen exit. They couldn't believe their luck: free food and drinks and they were first in!

The evening wore on. The alcohol held out, but the food didn't, despite the chef's team emptying the cool rooms and cooking everything in sight. Behind the bar, the drip trays—the aluminium trays under the beer taps that catch any overflow beer—had been emptied three times. Each time they were emptied, a purple–blue ethyl dye solution had to be sloshed in, so that the contaminated waste was tipped out after it had been measured. This was a health directive and was strictly enforced by the health inspectors, because in the old days before dye, it was tipped back into the kegs and resold as a "heart-starter".

As a note of interest, Jean, my mother-in-law, told me about the heart-starter. The nip measures for spirits, a silver cup-like pourer that held one nip, 50ml, or half a nip, 25ml, also had to be upended over a tray of ethyl dye; but before this was law, the leftover spirits from the untreated drip tray were emptied into a special bottle. This bottle was kept for the alcoholics who were first through the doors when they opened. One shot of this, their hearts started again, and the trembling in their hands stopped—hence the name heart-starter!

This night, as the trays were emptied, the bottle holding the dye (made by mixing ethyl dye tablets and water) was empty. "I'll get you some," a useful told the barmaid as he bent down to the cupboard under the sink and put the large plastic bottle containing the tablets on the top of the bar. He then showed some initiative. Somewhere, somehow, in the adrenaline of the night, he must have thought, *this could happen again tonight.* So, he tipped out enough tablets to fill a saucer and left it on top of the bar above the sink.

Meanwhile, our merry little barflies at the ends of the bar missed this. They were too busy watching the kitchen for the next tray of food to come out. After grabbing a bit more food as the waitress passed by, they turned to the bar and their eyes lit up.

"Look guys," chortled John, one of the Greedy Eight. "They've even got some lollies for us!"

"Best place ever, this," enthused Allan.

With that, the Greedy Eight jostled for the saucer and managed to grab a handful each. They swallowed them. Next minute—pandemonium. They were frothing at the mouth. Their lips were blue. They looked at each other and started screaming blue murder. And then stopped, stunned. Eight pairs of eyes had seen eight sets of blue teeth! I have never seen men part a crowd so quickly and head for the gents—rocket-propelled. I have never known men to stay in a toilet so long or to come out with their lips so tightly pressed together!

These guys had no hope of picking up a sheila at Sheila's that night!

Calcutta Day

Sheila's 1985. Calcutta Day. A Calcutta was a betting game played before the Melbourne Cup. It was held on the Monday before the Cup, after the field of 24 runners was known.

It went like this: It was in three parts. The first part, held two days before the Melbourne Cup, determined the owner of a horse and how much he paid for it.

The second part, Calcutta Day (the day before the Melbourne Cup), determined how much the bidder paid for it. The third part, Melbourne Cup day itself, was dividing the pot of winnings after the Cup had been run.

This was the first part. The Cup field was written on a large whiteboard. The starting price was written on the left-hand side of the board beside the name of each horse. On the right-hand side, beside the horse's name, a space was left. This was to write in the "owner" of the horse. (This owner did not own the horse until he bought it at the bidding the next day.) In those days it cost $200 to be in the draw to become an owner. This was determined by a draw out of a hat. The auctioneer first drew out a person's name from one hat, and then drew a horse's name from the other. All the owners' money was put in the pot.

On Calcutta Day, the bidding for the Cup field started.

On Melbourne Cup day, when the result of the Cup was known, the owner of the first horse took 70 per cent of the pot, second took 15 per cent of the pot, and third took 10 per cent—the owner of the horse that came last taking 5 per cent.

On this particular Calcutta Day, the sun was shining on the rear roof garden of the tavern. The tables and chairs, and the plants, had been pushed back to make maximum room for the punters. The staff were in jockey silks—red and black, purple and pink, green and white—complete with jockeys' caps! Brian stood out in his straw boater, red polka-dot bow tie and red-and-white-striped blazer. Sam the Seed, the auctioneer, was standing on a milk crate and was resplendent in his yellow-and-black paisley-embroidered jerkin, black top hat perched jauntily on his head. Tricky Dickie the Penciller—more formally dressed in his undertaker's black tails and red-and-black-banded straw boater—was standing beside Sam, with his Texta held ready to record the bets. The punters filled the beer garden: John the Bank Manager, Phantom and Dashing Don from Water Resources, Dave the Repossession Man—they were all there, schooners in hand, ready to bet for the big one, the winner of the Melbourne Cup ("The race that stops a nation"). In those days it really did: very few went back to work!

On this Calcutta Day, the syndicates gathered to buy the horse they thought would win. Some of the horses were bought for thousands, as the punters would form syndicates with names like "The Dirty Dozen", "The Winners", "She's Spent", "The

Bankies", "The Legal Wigs", "Mum's Choice" and many others. It was a good move to buy a horse. If you were the successful bidder for that horse and the owner of the horse, you would pay only half the bid price (so if it was bid up to $600, you would only pay $300). Of course, the punters might bid up the horse, especially with the help of Brian the Publican—the more money in the pot, the greater the crowd drawn on Melbourne Cup day.

"How much am I bid for What a Nuisance?" called Sam the Seed briskly, "Starting at 33–1. Dig deep, gentlemen, she's better than that price suggests." I liked that one. It had run the distance. The jockey, Pat Hyland, was okay, the weight was right. At its long odds, the blokes reckoned that I could have it as I didn't know what I was doing.

"$50. $100. Thanks, Bob. $200 from Lyn, the publican's wife. $500 from Brian the Publican."

Does he know something we don't? the crowd must have thought.

"Going once; going twice ... Knocked down to Brian the Publican for $500."

Tricky Dickie wrote up my name.

In an aside, Brian the Publican said to me, "I bought it for you, love, to keep the pot going. It hasn't got a hope."

"Now, ladies and gentlemen, the favourite, Our Sophia, starting at 9–2." The Phantom looked at his mates. They had a secret betting syndicate with a $2,000 pot, but Brian the Publican knew about their pot! He was going to make them bet to the max. Brian's mate, Johnno, was trying to give him the nod that this was the bet to keep going. He didn't need any nod! He took them up to $2,050 for the horse before another punter entered the field. The new punter figured that 10 per cent of what looked like a huge win for himself wasn't much. (The golden rule of the Calcutta is that the winning owner of the horse puts 10 per cent of his win on the bar for the rest of the punters to drink out.)

Beauty! thought Brian the Publican, deliberating the money in the till, "*If this keeps going, the money on the bar will mean a huge drink!*"

Sam the Seed was happy. He could see a long bidding race, with free schooners coming throughout the Calcutta. He kept it going.

Ten minutes later: "Any more bids?" Down crashed his black cane. Roll on free schooners! And so the fun continued. Record prices paid to own Kiwi and Mapperley Heights (both at 8–1: equal second favourites), and Tristarc (9–1).

Calcutta Day is exciting, but the Melbourne Cup is yet to come. All the boys will be there for the whole of Cup afternoon. Already, workers from the offices around have drawn lots as to who will have to go back at 4 p.m. to bundy off for their mates. A bundy clock was a card machine that measured your working hours. You bundied in when you started work (put your card in the machine and had your starting time recorded) and you bundied off when you finished. Of course, the pundits (slang for bosses) didn't know whether the worker was there or not without a physical check. Mates really were mates in those days.

Another great long lunch had ended. Diane, 65, nicknamed The Boiler because of her age—most people thought she was Brian the Publican's mother and that he was a slave driver—was having a middy of Old as she made sure all the tables were cleared again for the afternoon rush. The syndicate members would soon be back for their afternoon drink before home. The glorious days of the '80s were alive and well: no breathalyser, a few drinks at lunchtime, all AOK.

The next day, Cup Day, saw all the happy punters lined up, schooners in hand once more, to watch the Cup on the two giant video screens. There was a bit of added excitement for this Cup. It was the first time the Cup had been sponsored with prize money of $1 million. Fosters Brewery was the inaugural sponsor with the added attraction of another first—"Fashions on the Field". Brian, canny Publican that he was, had a few kegs donated from the brewery for the punters. More free drinks. Charles and Diana were the royal guests. No less important in our eyes, was another guest, Leanne Edelsten, who was a Sheila's patron.

And now the result of that Cup. To the great dismay of all the "professional" punters, and after all the underhand secrecy of syndicates, I won the Calcutta! I was very happy as I put my money—10 per cent of my winnings—over the bar for them to drink out. The "Legal Wigs" bought Under Oath. It is still coming. They wouldn't have fared any better with Lacka Reason. Our Sophia, the favourite, and a no-risk bet as far as "The Bankies" were concerned, came tenth.

You can imagine the "professional" punters' comments when a woman won the money, but because she had done the right thing, all was soon forgiven and forgotten.

BEHIND THE BAR-ROOM DOOR

My Mate Bernice

Throughout my years at the Union Hotel at North Sydney and especially during my days at Sheila's, I had a good mate—Bernice. Bernice and I met when our kids were at St Mary's Primary School in Ridge Street, North Sydney. Her daughter Briony was the same age as my daughter, Kate. (Briony was the little girl Kate met on the first day of kindergarten.)

Bernice's son, Dylan, and my son, "Buddha", also became firm friends. Budds was so nicknamed because he was rotund, but on being asked at St Joseph's College, Hunter's Hill, the origin of his nickname, he swiftly replied, "It's because I pray a lot!" Went down a treat at that school! Anyway, Dylan and Budds became best mates. The children used to play upstairs together at the hotel after school until Bernice arrived to pick up Dylan and Briony. Bernice and I became good mates after an incident at St Mary's.

One morning I arrived at the school to hear an altercation coming from around the side of the church where the mothers used to park.

"You can't park here again," said an elderly male voice.

"Why not?" replied an irate female voice.

I think that's Bern, I said to myself as I rounded the corner, all guns blazing. My paternal grandmother was a suffragette and the fight to right all wrongs comes out strongly in me, so strongly that I think all my grandmothers, maternal and paternal, from way back must have been suffragettes! I came around the corner to find Bern and an old priest standing toe to toe.

"What do you mean she can't park here? She's a working mother! She has two children to support on her own. She can't afford parking fees!"

"I don't care," said the old priest.

"Don't worry, Bern," I said, "you can park in the hotel car park."

So started our friendship! I'd like to relate a few instances from our history that will explain why we became good mates. One of the customers at Sheila's was a lovely girl called Janne. We had arranged to have a night out with her and met up at the bottom bar at Sheila's about 8pm. Brian the Publican was being an angel again and minding all the kids. We had a couple of drinks there and decided to go to the San Francisco Grill at the Hilton for dinner. The Hilton was an institution in those days. It had the Marble Bar, which is still there, and the San Francisco Grill ("the Grill"), which did not survive the 2005 renovation.

The San Francisco Grill was famous for its silver service. This is a form of service whereby waiters serve the main course dishes at the table from a silver platter. They served the meal to your plate, already in place in front of you, from the left side and cleared from the right. You had to remember to lean slightly to the right when serving was in progress and to the left during plate-clearing! They also had Gueridon Service. This was a cartwheeled to your table for speciality dishes to be cooked in front of you, or, in the case of cheese or bread, for you to make selections from it. Two dishes that were famous for Gueridon-style preparation were Chateaubriand, a beef fillet that was finished off and carved in front of you, and Crepe Suzette, a pancake that was sauced, flamed, and also served in front of you. This may sound very grand, and it was, but the "pièce de résistance" was the signature dish. A small silver tray in the shape of the San Francisco Bridge was presented with coffee. On it had been placed dry ice, which produced the mist of San Francisco Bay , and on this were four or five chocolate-coated peppermint ice-cream balls! This was Sydney in the days of Romano's, Pruniers, the Silver Spade Room, The Coachmen. Dining was an event that you anticipated, dressed for and thoroughly enjoyed. The guests around you were often as varied and colourful as the menu.

We decided to have a pre-dinner drink at the cocktail bar outside the Grill. We were all dressed up and looked very attractive, even if I say it myself! We had been seated for a while with our martinis in front of us, and had polished off about three, when a guy who had been sitting at the end of the bar, moved up and asked if he could join us. He was closest to Janne, so she politely replied, "No. We are having a quiet drink and a chat and would appreciate it if you would go away."

No chance.

After retreating for a while and keeping his eyes fastened on the three of us, he thought he would try again.

"No," said Janne. "We have told you that we are having a quiet drink. We do not want to be disturbed."

The third time he tried, he said nothing. He perched on the stool beside Janne. He was ignored. Then he tried to join in our conversation. Janne very quietly gave us a wink and then opened her handbag and casually laid it on the bar between herself and the pest.

The guy went white, spluttered in his drink and knocked the heavy bar chair over in his haste to get away. Bernice and I looked at his retreating figure, looked at Janne and laughed.

"How did you manage that, Janne?" asked Bernice.

Janne gave a little smile and pushed her open handbag over to us. Inside it was a pistol.

It wasn't only blokes who were part of the underworld!

Often, we would go to the Bourbon and Beefsteak—the safest place in the Cross. The Bourbon was another Sydney institution, particularly in the '60s when it opened. It was rumoured that it had been set up by the American Government and also rumoured that the boss there, Bernie, was CIA. His job was to garner any intelligence he could from the American servicemen who were on leave from Vietnam, a view also reinforced by the rumour that he would fly out of Richmond Air Force Base to Washington once a year in a StarLifter—a large American cargo plane.

The Bourbon was very American—there was bourbon, of course, and the best hamburgers in town! It introduced Australia to the American way of eating: salads before a meal, water before and during a meal. However, it could not get us drinking water. The Australian attitude was "Waste of good drinking time" or "It will rust your insides", or the most horrific thought of all, "Fish wee in it".

When you walked in, there was a large eating area on the right, all tables dressed with dazzling white tablecloths. There was a Maître d' in a black dinner jacket ready to show you to your table where a very large menu, in size and selection, was gently placed in your hands while the napkin was equally gently laid across your lap. Very classy. A little further on and to the left was a long bar, stools all along, placed just perfectly for conversation that was not meant to be overheard. Then tables and a good-sized dance floor. The best feature, in many opinions—and the one that stands out clearly in most patrons' memories—was a piano at the end of the bar with enough space for people to sit around and drink, usually American cocktails. The pianist played jazz, generally the popular kind—Ella Fitzgerald, Tony Bennett, Frank Sinatra. The Bourbon was the place to be and such fun!

I started going there in the '60s when Sydney girls went out with the visiting servicemen. Usually you met at the American Club, which held dances to facilitate meetings. It was unheard of for a "nice" girl to meet any American in a bar! The Cross went all out to cater for these boys, with strip clubs, gambling dens and brothels. There were drugs, but they were something that was unknown to the average young Australian, who would not have known what they looked like or if an exchange was happening. The American male also brought super good manners when taking out a girl and always gave them a gift on first meeting. In hindsight, I can understand the furore during World War II, when the

Australian men got upset when the girls flocked to the servicemen then! "Overpaid, oversexed and over here."

Bernice and I often went to the B&B and felt extremely comfortable. In the '80s, instead of servicemen there were all types—underworld personalities, police, regulars from the Cross, hospitality employees, property developers... anyone really. We were lucky enough to know many of them, from big Renee, the doorman, to most of the clientele. We wouldn't get there until after midnight and the place was buzzing.

This night, Bern and I sat at the bar in our usual seats and ordered our usual drinks—Scotch and soda for Bern, martini for me. For some reason, we never had to pay for our drinks. We put it down to being in the hospitality business (Sheila's was raging at that time), but I think that it was due more to the fact that we knew most of the goodies and baddies in town!

We began chatting to the barman and to the people next to us, and, as one does, got into an interesting conversation. The fellow next to me admired my engagement ring.

"There's a lovely stone in that," he said.

"Yes," I replied, "I'm giving it to my older daughter. I have two daughters. I would love to find another one of the same size for my other daughter."

With that he whipped out his notebook.

"I'll just take details," he said. "What size is it, and what clarity?"

So I went along with this and told him. When he wanted my contact information, I realised he was serious.

"Thanks," I said. "Let me think about it and I'll let you know next time I see you up here."

"No worries," he said, "I know what you want. I can get it overnight and you'll have it the next day."

It was a common thing for "people in the know" to order things that would be stolen to suit. I didn't want to be part of any shady deals, but I knew a bloke who did. His particular band of mates specialised in stealing clothes. One day this bloke was passing through Coffs Harbour on his way to see his parents on the Gold Coast. He was walking along a Coffs street when he passed his two mates disguised in white overalls wheeling a large clothes-stand jammed with men's suits. They winked at him, not a word was exchanged, and the guys went whistling along on their merry way. Another placed order, another satisfied customer!

It was a "wink and a nod" type of society. There were boundaries between the criminals and the citizens and people generally stayed within them; however, it was also as if there was osmosis, and sometimes one could slip in and out without any harm.

Barry the Basher

Sheila's fulfilled a community function, as all hotels and taverns did in those days. The difference between a hotel and a tavern then was that the tavern had to have food available during all their opening hours and the licensee did not have to live on the premises. Hotels, on the other hand, did not have to have food available during all opening times and the licensee usually lived on the premises. In the spirit of this requirement, we often had lunchtime entertainment and patrons often stayed on all afternoon and into the night.

Once a week we would have a high-class fashion parade compered by Carol Provan, the footballer's wife. Whilst it was beautifully and professionally staged, the models were the main attraction, for the men at least. On this day, our front of house manager, Mrs Lewis, aka "The Boiler", had done her usual magnificent job of arranging tables and group bookings. You messed with Mrs Lewis at your own peril. She had been a hostess at Romano's in her heyday, and did not appreciate the groups that ogled the models rather than appreciating the clothes and the professionalism with which Carol presented her show.

Mrs Lewis was 5 feet tall (152 cm) and weighed about seven

stone (44.5 kg) wringing wet, but she had ways of ruling with an iron fist. To an ogling offender she would say, "I'm sorry, Jim, your booking came in too late for a close seat. I had to put you down the back." As there were generally 300 patrons seated for these shows, this was punishment indeed, and that the show was simultaneously recorded on the large video screens was no compensation!

All tables, those beside the catwalk and those down the back, were looked after by Billy Peiker, wine waiter extraordinaire, at that time about 60 years of age and still a stylish man. Billy was also a professional, and very savvy. He looked after the patrons really well, and consequently got plenty of tips, particularly as the afternoon wore on and the punters became merrier. Table service of wine ceased after 4 p.m. and it was necessary to go to the bar or the bottle shop to purchase your own. Billy's favourites never had to do this. Although he had finished his shift and was having his usual schooner of VB with Mrs Lewis, who favoured her middy of Old, he would shuffle over to the wine shop to personally bring them their favourite wine.

It was after one such lunchtime fashion parade that Barry the Basher decided to stay on. Barry was a local North Shore boy who played footy for the Neutral Bay Packers, but the Packers had no inkling of what Barry could really pack. They thought that it was only in the scrum! Barry was a tall, good-looking bloke whose physical prowess as a "persuader" was in demand. He could reel in the sheilas, and his lisp only made him more adorable; he was a great big teddy bear of a bloke—to some. If a job had to be done, the word around town was, "Barry's your man!" He was pretty good with his fists, and if you were lucky enough to be Barry's mate, he was protective of you, too. Our bar manager Peter wasn't one of his mates. Bernice was.

Barry the Basher had been having a drink at the luncheon show and had moved with his female companion to the easy-chairs closer to the bar for a few more. They were enjoying their Moët et Chandon so much, they decided to have another bottle. However, Barry was not impressed when he was told that he would have to get up and get his own champagne. He called for the manager.

"What do you mean I can't be served here?" demanded Barry. Peter, a nervous sort of bloke, and knowing who he was, stuttered the rules. With that, Barry jumped up, tipping over what was left of his champagne, pulled a gun and pointed it at Pete. Barry the Basher started to make his demands:

"Mate, I want champagne and I want it now!" But he was talking to thin air. Pete had fainted at Barry's feet and had to be carted away and revived. Needless to say, Barry got his table service!

When I got in the next day, I wasn't happy. I heard about the incident and called Peter into the office.

"What is wrong with you?" I asked. "Why didn't you take the gun off him and bar him? I would have done that, and I would have expected you to as well."

Peter just looked at me.

"Lyn, I didn't want to end up another casualty." I saw his point.

About six months later, Bernice arrived at Sheila's about 11 a.m., an unusual time for her. She was dressed in a subdued suit, high heels and had a strange look on her face.

"What are you doing here?" I asked, "You're all dressed up. Where have you been?"

"I've been to Barry the Basher's funeral," she replied.

By all accounts it was a big funeral, with people from all walks of life coming to farewell Barry, some of them with great relief. Some were recognisable: prostitutes from the Cross, newspaper "celebrities" and a lot of unknown "colourful" characters.

Bernice was still naïve in many ways. She thought these unknown characters—the guys in black suits—were part of the choir, come to send off Barry on a nice note. They probably were the ones who did send him off. And who they actually were remains a mystery to this day.

I did hear the rumour of his manner of passing. Very professional. Barry loved a good long lunch with a good few ales, a good few bottles of wine. He got an invitation he couldn't refuse. A mate invited him to a long lunch at a swish harbourside restaurant in the eastern suburbs. His driver would pick him up in a long, sleek, black Jaguar. Barry was in. He couldn't resist. But what he didn't know was that the driver was a professional racing car driver and his job was not to deliver Barry safely to the long lunch.

He hopped in at the top of William Street, below the Coca-Cola sign, all spiffed up—striped pale-blue shirt, cream trousers, deck shoes and a huge anticipatory grin. He shot off in style, sizzled along to Bayswater Road and straight into a telegraph pole. Poor old Barry was done, but, miracle of miracles, the driver got not a scratch.

It pays to know a bit about the bloke who gives you a lift.

Sheila's Coasters

This was the '80s. People seemed to get on pretty well. If they didn't, they said so. Probably a good thing. We had the most interesting coasters in town, thanks to the combined brains and imagination of some of the guys at the Union Hotel at North Sydney.

One afternoon, while Sheila's was still in the planning stages, Kevin, Stan, and Brian the Publican were in the Corner Bar discussing the exciting new prospect that was to be Sheila's.

"What are you doing about coasters, Brian?" asked Kevin.

"Oh, I suppose I'll get them from the brewery for free," answered Brian.

"No, mate," said Kevin. "I think we should design some."

I was walking by at this point and Kevin said, "What's the colour, Lyn?"

"Shocking pink," I answered.

With that, we decided that the front logo should feature a rose, a big picture hat, and a lady's hand holding a champagne glass. We thought that would say it all. Stan and Kevin got to work. Pretty soon they had enlisted two other mates—Bruce and Alan from J&K Printing. At that time, coasters only had printing on one side. I clearly remember Kevin picking up a coaster from the bar and saying, "There should be something on the back. You always turn a coaster over."

So were born "The Ladies of Sheila's". Today, in our politically correct society, these coaster slogans would never see the light of day:

"Turn me over for a good time."

"Climax your week at Sheila's."

"Sheila's, the best pick-up in town."

"Complicate your life at Sheila's."

"Girls do it at Sheila's."

"Where the boys are."

All coaster slogans were accompanied by "appropriate" images. I will leave some of those images and slogans to your imagination. Maybe some of you will remember more.

There were 20 in total. They were very popular and became collector's items. Within the first six months, 400,000 had been printed. It cost a fortune in postage to send them to collectors in Australia and overseas, but they epitomised the spirit of Sheila's: "Naughty but Nice".

TAVERN
RESTAURANT
NIGHT SPOT

For reservations
Phone: 922 7489

sheila's

77 Berry Street, North Sydney

Sheila's would like to thank Stan, Kevin, Bruce and Alan for their innovative coaster designs.

They added so much to the magic that was Sheila's.

The Sheila Had a Good Side

It was turning out to be a huge night. The size of Sheila's and its popularity as flavour of the year meant that it was in high demand for charity fundraising. The advertising agencies, radio stations 2UE and 2GB, and the television stations got behind the nights. There was always a crowd of 2,000 people, all ready to bid for works of art for auction.

At one event, the works ranged from a large Lloyd Rees etching, to cartoons and special pieces submitted and framed by the agencies. At 2 p.m. that day, the agencies sent in workmen, who assembled large easels to display the work. These pieces were displayed from 3 p.m. Naturally, the rest of the agency people arrived in good time for the auction, usually 4 p.m. They felt that "a good glow up" was essential to ensure maximum prices achieved. They achieved the glow up and so did the rest of the crowd.

By 7 p.m., the place was full. There were people sitting or leaning everywhere, all engaged in animated, vital conversations. Then the auctioneer, an estate agent's auctioneer, arrived and the place was set to buzz. Large amounts were raised for the charity involved, because all services and works of art were donated.

Sheila's did not charge room hire for any event, and were probably the first to begin a trend that continued in the hospitality industry for a while. It was not necessary to charge because of the money generated from alcohol sales over the bar. The auctioneer donated his services, the artists and agencies donated their artwork.

These events happened yearly, for about ten years, with different agencies organising the event for a charity of their choice.

The Children's Hospital, then at Camperdown, benefited yearly to the tune of $100,000, which was a huge amount in the '80s. I remember that Brian and I were given a beautiful commemorative medal as a thank you when the hospital moved to Westmead. After the Oliver Twist Committee Fundraiser organised for the Prince of Wales Children's Hospital, we received a letter dated 10 December 1984, extending "our thanks and appreciation to you and compliments to the chef for the excellent food he supplied for the night". And it was excellent food. Bob Stone, the Executive Chef, had been the Executive Chef at the Savoy, London.

On 14 April 1993, the Starlight Foundation raised enough money with their fashion parade to grant the wishes of many children, one of whom was a little girl with a brain tumour who wished for a dog. The Multiple Sclerosis society also benefited— the money raised going towards a vehicle to assist people who resided at the MS Centre, to access the local community. There were many times that donations for prizes were given to North Sydney Council for their Senior Citizens days. A popular prize was Sheila's Shiraz Cabernet, which we had specially bottled with our own pink label. It sold for $6.50 a bottle in '84. It was probably the first time a venue had bottled their own wine under their own label.

There was one "charity" event that caused me personal abuse. Apparently, one of the sponsors of this event had been duped, just as we had.

I was attending a Cornell University marketing seminar at the Hilton in Brisbane and a young would-be executive, surrounded by mates, erupted,

"What do you think you mean by making a fool of me?"

"What do you mean?" I asked.

"That '87 Fat Girls' Quest. We thought that it was legitimate and we sponsored it. You made a fool of us."

"Look here," I said, "The venue was hired to stage a beauty pageant. You should have checked out the company before you rushed in to sponsor. The prejudging to select 87 girls was held at Bankstown Square; the final was held at Sheila's. You were fooled, as was everyone, and if it makes you look bad with your bosses that is your problem."

The "87 Fat Girls" Quest was one of the slickest promotions I have ever seen. The MC was Jacko—"I'm an individual, you can't fool me!"—of Energizer battery ad fame. In his previous life, Jacko had been an AFL player of note, having represented Melbourne, St Kilda and Geelong, and having played 82 games for 308 goals. A legend.

The finalists arrived on the night of Friday, 27 June 1987, to parade in the contest that had been advertised as "The alternative Miss Australia Quest". The girls had to be over 70kg, and have a

133

bust measurement of 97 centimetres or over. To get to the finals stage, the girls completed a form that asked for their vital statistics, their occupation, and what they considered to be the most interesting thing about them. They also agreed to be photographed or interviewed if they won or were placed. The team who organised this must have had a sense of humour. All three winners were given a cash amount from "Miracle Bra, the bra for bigger women" plus modelling representation from the Kilos Plus Model Agency. The winner of first place had an extra bonus—"The winner's weight in scorched peanuts from Colonial Chocolate Company".

If the unhappy executive had read the form properly, he would have realised it was a spoof. Doesn't say much for his brains or the company that employed him.

The night arrived. The girls were cheerful and knew each other. They wore whatever they wanted and all looked lovely. The big moment arrived. Finalists lined up. Jacko's spoof. Fanfare. Lights pulsing.

Instead of the finalists parading, a group of young guys, some carrying musical instruments, bounded onto the stage. "87 Fat Girls" was a band.

After some stunned silence, there was lots of laughter, much of it coming from the beauty contestants themselves. The girls were shouted an endless supply of champagne from Sheila's special bottles with the trademark pink lady on the front. The girls were good sports. They voted it one of the best nights they had had.

And the band wasn't too bad either.

Rock 'N' Rollin' Sheila's—With Apologies to Col Joye's 'Clementine'

Entertainment was what Sheila's was all about—from the dance floor to the antics of the patrons—whether it was manoeuvres to chat up the opposite sex or watching the antics on the dance floor.

The disco area was bounded by four large glass pillars. There would have been over three thousand people "cutting up" the marble dance floor every night.

One particular incident late at night on that dance floor stands out in my memory.

"Brian, come and have a look at the antics of your mate."

Beer in hand, Brian the Publican wandered over. The silver disco ball in the middle of floor was spinning. Multicoloured lights from above were pirouetting on the floor. Patrons were busy making all kinds of moves. There he was, fawn gabardine overcoat swirling around as he danced with the "good sort" opposite. Only trouble was the "good sort" was his own reflection in one of the four square glassed columns. An image that, to this day, is not forgotten.

Patrons made all kinds of efforts to be part of the scene. Of course, you could enter in the traditional way, through the front door. But one guy made a more spectacular entrance.

Crowie and our weekend manager, Michael, were out in the back conservatory, Crowie having a beer, Michael being conscientious and listening while his eyes darted around to make sure all was as it should be. They spotted a bloke clambering over the back wall and dropping to the ground. Now this was no ordinary feat. To get to the conservatory, this bloke would have had to have climbed up the brick wall from the lane three storeys below. Michael and Crowie fronted him.

"How did you do that, mate?" asked Crowie. "It's three floors."

"I do a bit of climbing," the bloke replied. A bit of an understatement.

"What do you want me to do, Crowie?" asked Michael as he prepared to escort him to the front door and put him out.

Crowie laughed. "For a bloke who's that keen to get in, and can't because the queue's too long, hell, buy him free drinks all night!"

Entertainment was the name of the game from day one. At midday and 5 p.m. each day, Kevin Somerville, pianist extraordinaire, would begin playing our oddest entertainment fixture—a hot-pink baby grand. I thought he did a really good job, but this entertainment didn't last long. For one thing, you couldn't hear it because of the sheer chatter of the 600 lunchtime patrons and the clink of their wine glasses; and at 5 p.m. it was time to start partying after work, so the noise had a more raucous sound. It was with deep regret that we pensioned off the piano and let the place "rock'n'roll" instead.

Rock'n'roll it did. We had some great bands and acts booked by David Jacobsen, as it was a top venue, well-equipped and with its own band room where the bands could relax with their riders. Mostly they wanted beer, bourbon with mixers, Scotch, rarely wine, rarely soft drink, although one singer always wanted a bottle of port to "warm up the vocal cords". I used to get furious with these riders as I thought since I was paying for them to perform, they could pay for their own drinks. If I was on duty they often did. They were okay if Brian was there.

Col Joye said to me one day, "What are you worried about, Lynnie? Some of the international acts we bring out want cases of a special champagne, dozens of a particular kind of spirit. Our fellas don't want too much at all." Perspective.

We didn't know it, but we were close to the end of the entertainment era in Sydney. Big entertainment venues started closing at the end of the '90s. I imagine there were a lot of factors—insurance, smoke, noise, cost—but at this time the scene was strong.

Sheila's entertainment was diverse. As well as singing groups from Australia and overseas, there were comedians such as Vince Sorrenti, Austen Tayshus and Steady Eddy on the week's comedy night. Col Joye also introduced overseas acts such as Chubby Checker, and invited into Sheila's overseas artists and friends who were performing in, or visiting Australia. These personalities from music, TV and films helped draw a crowd.

Sometimes overseas guests had difficulty getting in the door. This was early days and the staff were new. It was a surprise for one doorman to meet Col Joye and George Hamilton at the entrance.

"I'm Col Joye, and this is George Hamilton," Col said as he approached the door.

"And I'm the Pope," replied Big Paddy, the Irish doorman.

Colin and George lined up. Ha! It took them an hour to get in.

Our lunchtime fashion parades started as a Melbourne Cup parade, and then became regular events. Later we had a tasteful lingerie parade, and then a not-so-tasteful mud-wrestling contest.

Our video screens are also worth a mention. They were the first and the largest two video screens in Australia. They showed the latest hits. There were Bryan Ferry videos, and *Flashdance ... What a Feeling.* Videos played all day and night unless dance music was playing. Some of the songs I remember include *Tell Her About It,* Billy Joel; *What's Love Got to Do with It,* Tina Turner; *Born in the U.S.A.,* Bruce Springsteen; *Wham Rap! (Enjoy What You Do),* Wham!—and, of course, my theme song, *December, 1963 (Oh, What a Night),* sung by Frankie Valli and The Four Seasons!

There were sporting events on the video screens, too. In 1983, the biggest sporting event was the America's Cup. There had been a lot of controversy over the winged keel designed by Ben Lexcen. This controversy, combined with the flamboyant nature of Alan Bond, created unprecedented interest. The place was packed. The race was on both video screens.

It was the first time in 132 years that the Americans had lost the Cup. The patrons took their lead from our Prime Minister, Bob Hawke, who famously said, "Any boss who sacks anyone for not turning up today day is a bum." They stayed all day from 11 in the morning. Very few went back to work.

One of Sydney's leading fight promoters, Bill Mordey, used the venue and the video screens to promote fights from around the world. Some lasted 20 to 60 minutes; one only lasted about ten seconds. There was a $20 admission for this, even though this short, ten-second fight was out of our control. Sheila's was full of blokes. They had just sat down with their beers and were ready to settle in. The fight started. The fight ended.

"Brian," I said, "we'll have to give them their meal for free. They will get nothing for their money." Brian disagreed—that was the luck of the draw—but I had the announcement made. In retrospect, it probably wasn't such a bad idea. The alcohol sales were good and most of them stayed until mid-afternoon and into the night.

Sheila's was a great place. I believe it was the prototype for later venues, as it was a place where people could meet safely and it had a social conscience. It was the ideal venue to raise money for charity and I am proud that we could be part of that. But I think that it is best remembered as a fun place whose opening slogan was "The place to be in '83". Then, they came "Back for more in '84".

Sheila's Blokes

Brian the Publican always said, "Where the ladies are, the blokes are," and how right he was. The girls flocked in, all dressed to the nines, and the boys followed even faster. We had young, single, attractive blokes, and middle-aged blokes who still thought they had it, and perhaps some did. (There is something attractive about a good-looking, 40-something bloke.) Then there were the "red-eye specials". I call them this because they could be any age, and the yellow eyeballs with red road maps gave away one of the loves of their lives. We also had the older "sophisticates"—well-dressed, well-heeled and with well-brushed egos. We had hospitality workers, advertising types, bankers, television and radio person-alities. They were all there. Sheila's was the place to be.

There was the bloke who took a "shine" to me, or maybe I was putting his attention on a higher plane than it deserved. It didn't matter that The Boiler knew his name and game, and was always close by to keep an eye on him. It didn't matter that I was married and Brian was usually visible, or if not seen, heard, for he always had a good story to tell and an audience to tell it to.

This day the bloke bought his Scotch and soda, and as I was standing near the bar, he asked me if I would like a drink.

Well, is the Pope a Catholic? Of course I said yes. I had about half an hour before Brian was due to come back from taking the kids to sport, to pick me up. The Boiler was having a middy and a Winnie Red with Bill the Wine Waiter. Our friend thought he was safe, No such luck. The Boiler's glittering, beady eyes shrivelled. She was on alert!

He started with the line that was guaranteed to win any girl's heart. "You're not a bad sort."

Okay. Right. Nice. Sip of red wine. Another swallow of Scotch and soda. Where is this going? "Thank you," I commented.

Repeat. "You're not a bad sort... but there is one thing. Why don't you take elocution lessons and learn to speak without that accent? You're not in the bush now."

I took another sip. He took another sip, pleased with himself.

"Why don't you finish your drink?" I said. "You're barred."

I still have a bush accent. No one has tried to improve my elocution again.

I forgot to mention that we even had a sheik. Thanks to Crowie. God knows where he dredged this bloke up, but suddenly there he was. In front of me. I was in the same area, at the bottom bar. It was about 11 p.m. and I was serving a customer.

"Hi Lyn," says Crowie.

What a great excuse for me to stop work and have a convivial drink and chat. Crowie was, after all, a partner, and a good bloke. Then I noticed the fellow he was with. A good-looking, dark-skinned, very well-dressed person, obviously not your typical Aussie.

141

"Would you like a drink?" Crowie said, and then introduced me: "This is Omar."

They may have been blind—blind drunk, that is—but I wasn't. In the next instance, Crowie pushed Omar towards me. I pushed Omar back. Back and forth went Omar, swinging like a pendulum. Back and forth, back and forth, between the two of us. The grin never left his face, or Crowie's. Finally I managed to push him to one side where he leant lopsidedly against the bar.

"What the hell are you doing, Crowie? Who is this?"

"Lyn, I think you could be nicer to this bloke. He wants to go out with you. He likes blondes. He wants to give you a two-carat diamond—I've seen it—and then buy Sheila's."

I don't think so.

"What are you thinking? I don't want any two-carat diamond and I certainly don't want to go out with 'Omar', if that's his name, and we don't want to sell Sheila's. Best thing you both could do is try to stand here, have another beer and behave."

So they did. Anytime this antic is brought up, Crowie's face breaks into a huge grin. It is a great joke now, but he had me going there for a while.

Then there was the doorman, Bob, who thought that he was a ladykiller. He did a great job, was pleasant, knew everyone, and was tough enough to stop any fight as long as the other doorman, Paddy, was beside him. He could really handle himself if there had ever been a need. We nicknamed him "the Lover". (His mate was "the Fighter".) The Lover was convinced that many of these good sorts who came in fancied him, and he may have been right. One night, the Lover came up to Brian the Publican.

"Brian, do you think I could have a camera?"

"What do you want a camera for, mate?" asked Brian.

"Look Brian, you must understand how hard it is here on the door. All these good-looking sorts coming through the door, and I'm not a bad-looking bloke. Naturally, I ask some out and write down their names and addresses; but when I ring them up, I can't remember if the one I'm talking to is really Judy, Jane or Catherine. I usually get it mixed up and then I've got no hope. Now if I had a camera, I could take a picture of her, note down a few pertinent facts on paper with the name and address, and then I'd know I was talking to the right girl. I'd be right, mate. I wouldn't get any knockbacks then."

"Yes,' said Brian, "I see your point, but I don't think Lyn would—and she's sure to find out."

"You're right," said the crestfallen Lothario, and he returned glum-faced to the job. But guess what? The next good-looking sort walked in and he was a ray of sunshine again. Hope springs eternal.

The term "Sir Lunchalot" was popular before it was immortalised by the lengthy political Chinese banquets of the '80s and '90s and the political shenanigans of the 21st century. We had our Sir Lunchalots and they did the term justice. Sheila's drew the white-collar workers of North Sydney for what was common then, and known as "the long lunch". Government departments such as Water Resources did the tradition proud; bank employees had to be hauled in by their respective bosses and told "lunch is one hour, boys and girls". In fact, to reinforce this the banks would often book a long table of 60: one for the noon sitting, one for the 1 p.m. sitting. It expanded the meaning of the term "hot beds" (a bed vacated by one shift worker and then immediately occupied by another): we had hot chairs. But the real Lunchalot boys made them all look like workaholics. These guys, generally a core group of four, held very responsible jobs in four big corporations. They would get to work no later than 7 a.m., which meant that they got most of their paperwork, office administration and phone calls completed by 11 a.m. Their secretaries knew where to find them, but rarely were they interrupted in their pursuit of conviviality. The real business of the day began about noon. Today it would be called "networking", as three of these guys worked in interrelated industries, and the fourth was a public servant. I wasn't privy to the business discussed, but there seemed to be utmost amiability. Billy, the wine waiter, was kept busy. They were one of the groups that constantly interrupted him from his traditional afternoon schooners of VB with The Boiler. Mind you, the guys showed their appreciation handsomely.

So, I'm sure there was some business benefit to the lunches, but there definitely was a huge benefit to Sheila's and to Billy. The guys would often drink a dozen bottles of wine between noon and 8 p.m. before their drivers came to take them home. Their wives may not have been happy, but they had nothing to worry about other than inebriated spouses. These guys had principles and morals, and the attractive girls that were a feature of the place were simply that—female drinkers. Even the fashion parades did not distract them too much from their conviviality.

Not the same could be said for all patrons, but The Boiler didn't miss a beat. The weekly fashion parades that started with the inaugural Melbourne Cup parade in 1983 employed models from an agency in Neutral Bay. They were so popular, and the girls so professional and attractive, that they were held monthly, and then weekly. As well as high fashion parades, there were lingerie parades. These were extremely tasteful and well presented. A catwalk had been built for these fashion parades. This catwalk fed onto the front of the stage from the middle of the dancefloor. Tables were angled from the edge of the catwalk, spidering into the room. So, with the close proximity of the tables, there was a male testosterone rush to book early to get a close table. The males were well-behaved... except for one bloke on one occasion. (And he should have known better with the job he held.) He patted one of the girls on the butt as she paraded. The eagle eye of The Boiler missed nothing. She was furious and plotted revenge. When it came time for booking the next parade, he rang up and the Boiler answered.

"I have given you one of the best seats," she said, as she puffed on her Winnie Red and sipped on her Old. "You're on the edge of the catwalk." The joy expressed on the other end could be gauged from the look of pure glee on her face.

"What are you up to, Boiler?" I asked.

"I've got a little surprise planned for him. I'll tell you on the day." I knew better than to spoil her fun. She was the queen of bookings and all things to do with table decorations and allocation. So the big Friday arrived and it was soon my turn to chortle.

Eleven-thirty arrived. In marched the perpetrator and his mates, 12 in all. All spruced up. Naturally, they had a few ales with their mate Brian the Publican, who had no idea of what was in store for them. Pride bolstered, The Boiler showing the way, he strutted in with his mates to one of the "best" tables. Naturally, he was seated on the end nearest the catwalk. Then, unusually, The Boiler seemed to be fussing around at the sound desk, pointing to the spotlights, pointing to Brett, the in-house technician, who was nodding sagely. Then she wandered out to the band room, which doubled as a dressing room for the models on these days.

What is she up to? I wondered. But I had no time to think too much. With The Boiler so obviously preoccupied, I had her reservations book and was showing patrons to their tables.

Music. Lights. Hushed expectant patrons. Twelve-thirty. The parade began. The girls did their usual gorgeous job, parading beautiful fashion items—usually from *Lena's*, an exclusive dress shop in North Sydney Shopping World—then lingerie, and then performing the finale. For the finale, one stunning girl was in spectacular lingerie, and not too much of it. This was particularly appreciated. Then all spotlights abruptly went off. Suddenly, our mate was brilliantly floodlit with this girl on his knee for all to see. He couldn't afford to be seen this way, much less enjoying food and drink at a licensed tavern. The girl was quick on her feet, she was back on the catwalk, looking cool and collected. He was spluttering and fit to murder someone. Brian the Publican came to the fore, defusing the situation.

"Come and have a beer, mate. You look a bit hot under the collar."

Each week after the show had finished and the crowd had dispersed, Brian (always the thoughtful and bountiful host) would sit with the models and buy them Veuve or Moët. These sessions would commence around three o'clock and often last until 8 p.m. It got a bit hard to take after a time.

The police deserve a special mention of thanks. The place was very successful and taking a lot of money. This attracted the criminal element and high-class prostitutes. We didn't think along those lines, but the police did. In the first two weeks, they warned off four heavy criminals and prostitutes known to them. After this, they were willing to provide an escort to walk each day to the National Bank (a block away), and later the Commonwealth Bank (next door), when, and if, Brian remembered to call. I don't know if it was bravado, stupidity or forgetfulness, but those calls were rarely made. However, it was a place full of attractive girls and good music and was the "in" place to be, so the police often came to have a drink there after their shift before going home. This in itself was a deterrent, and we were never robbed. Apparently, the word around the underside of town was that "the cops are always there".

The nights the Queensland State of Origin team came for dinner and a few drinks were nights that our children, Danielle, Kate and Brian, and Bernice's children, Briony and Dylan, have never forgotten. We went to 6 p.m. mass at St Mary's, Miller Street, North Sydney, and then headed down the hill for dinner with the footballers. They never minded sitting eating with the kids, talking to them and signing autographs. To this day the kids remember meeting Wally Lewis, Alfie Langer, Paul Vautin, Darren Lockyer, Gene Miles, Mal Meninga and many others. They were their heroes, and although Brian supported Queensland, as he was born in Tenterfield, the kids were staunch Blues supporters. They would follow the results of the games and were downcast when Queensland won the first two of the three matches of the 1984 series. (1984 was the third State of Origin competition.) Brian was given a photo of the 1984 Queensland State of Origin Team, and for the time Sheila's existed it hung proudly on the wall. After dinner, the footballers enjoyed their night, many with a cigarette in one hand and a perpetual drink in the other. Brian the Publican stayed with them while Bernice and I took the children home. There were whispers of the good time had throughout the night, but I was not privy to that. I can only imagine.

The North Sydney Rugby League players also frequented Sheila's. Saturdays after the game was a special night. After they had been back to North Sydney Leagues Club for a few beers and a presentation, they headed back down to Sheila's, where all the action was. They were a great lot and I remember Greg Florimo, Les Kiss, Mark Graham... But there was one guy who was an explosive force. He was a six-foot guy, long brown hair to his collar, a great smile: a good style of bloke, who, as Brian the Publican put it, used to have plenty of luck with the sheilas. However, one Thursday night he turned up and before long had blotted his copy book. He spied a group of ten attractive girls, and, as was his wont, with utmost confidence in his charm and good looks, went over to see if he would "have any luck". He didn't. Whatever he said had an outcome he hadn't experienced before. The girl threw her drink over him.

Brian said, "Mate, I'm sorry, but you'll have to go. I don't know what you said, but those girls aren't happy with you."

"I'm sorry, Brian," he replied, undaunted, as he and Brian headed for the door and the trademark, well-lit, palm-fringed ramp that led to Berry Street. "Let me go back in and buy that girl a drink, and you have one with me. I bet I walk out with the girl who threw the drink over me."

Things didn't start out well.

"I don't want your apologies and I don't want a drink from you."

"Let him apologise and buy you one." Reasonable request from Brian's point of view and the head-nodding, eyes-beseeching footballer's point of view.

"Let him buy everyone a drink." Jim Beam and coke all round. Seemed reasonable to the red-blooded Aussie girlfriends. Brian the Publican bought everyone a drink and, in the case of the wronged girl, made it a double JB and coke. At the end of the night, the footballer walked out with that girl.

Sheila's blokes came from all walks of life and because of Sheila's went their many, sometimes shattered, ways. Some got married because of Sheila's; some were married at Sheila's; some were divorced because of Sheila's. But all still agreed that it was "the place to be in '83", and for a good many years after.

PART 4
McGETTIGAN'S
1992–1996

McGettigan's

Sheila's morphed into McGettigan's in October 1991, and is well-remembered by people who today are in their late 30s to early 40s. At that time, most of this group (carrying their birth certificates or bus passes to verify their age) were in their teens, aged 12 to 17. No one over 18 was allowed entry.

McGettigan's was best known for its supervised underage parties on a Friday night and was the venue for the first of the "HSC Results" parties in NSW, held in 1992. The HSC parties were an initiative of our daughter Kate and her friend Mel Kokodas.

A dedicated underage venue was first suggested as a trial by a New South Wales policeman, Barry, who did a lot of work with youth on the streets at the Cross, many of whom had just been released from detention.

"Lyn, Brian," he said, "there is a big need for a safe place for kids to go. Somewhere with supervision and without alcohol. For all kids, not just those with problems."

"Nights for teen dance but alcohol strictly out", reported the *Sydney Morning Herald*, on 8 October 1992:

A North Sydney nightclub has broken new ground by getting the support of police, council and the licensing courts to run weekly alcohol-free dance nights for under 18s … "The licensing courts have not done this before, have not allowed clubs to deregulate … but we have the support of North Sydney police and the Mayor, Gerry Nolan," Mrs McGettigan [said]. "Something has to be done to provide entertainment for the youngsters," she added … Mrs McGettigan said she and her husband would be on duty at the club to supervise the nights and would organise fleets of taxis to be there before the 12.30 a.m. closure. The club's doormen would see youngsters into the cabs. Once the teenagers are at the club they will not be allowed to have pass-outs to go on to the streets. But the club has a large garden at the back."

So McGettigan's was born, but we did not know what a minefield we would be walking into and what misconceptions it would produce, especially in the mind of one headmistress of a girls' school on the Lower North Shore. She was convinced it was a hellhole where drugs, alcohol, brawls and heaven knows what else would take place. It actually turned out to be a place where school kids, particularly those on the Lower North Shore, could meet in safety. It was securely policed by the management with the help of Bernice and the NSW police.

There were strict guidelines to be followed. McGettigan's was a tavern, except for this Friday night. As such, all alcohol had to be taken off the shelves and locked away, and the cupboard keys kept securely in the office. All alcohol signage had to be removed, including the beer signage on the taps, and the taps themselves had to be screwed off. The wine bar servicing the tavern that provided takeaway alcohol during the day was locked and darkened. The lights on all bar fridges behind the bar had to be turned off so that no alcohol or wine bottles were visible. The free- pour bottles suspended on shelves above the additive/soft drink dispensers had to be removed. The free-pour dispenser key had to be removed and also kept in the office. Behind the bar, only soft drink or water were available. No glass could be used, so we had fluorescent plastic glasses: yellow, green, orange and red. They were so popular, they soon disappeared. The happy company producing them had a steady flow of income. We were probably the first outlet to have plastic glasses.

The next issue was security. As we had some problem kids, we installed metal detectors so each child was checked as they came in. We did find knives. These were confiscated, the police outside alerted and the child questioned. It was much harder work than running an adult's tavern. However, it was the forerunner of underage parties throughout the state. Many of these underage blue light discos were run by local councils, and we went to many areas explaining the set-up and the measures taken to make them safe. One measure not considered by councils was the songs played. Songs have an effect on the behaviour of people. Hard, heavy beat songs tended to excite, so generally a maximum of four of these were played in a set, then a number of softer, slower songs to calm the mood down.

Security was of two types—family and employed. Family was Brian and me; our two older daughters, Kate, 16 and Danielle, 18;

Kate's mate Briony and her mother, Bernice. Physical security was a big thing. The guys employed had to be licensed security, but with experience dealing with kids—firm but not intimidating. We had the ideal people. They had worked security at Sheila's since we had opened. The most memorable and much-loved ones were two gentle giants: "The Grizzies". They always seemed to smile as they looked down from their great height. They were the first to greet the kids when they entered, and made a point of getting to know as many of the names as they could. As they patrolled inside the premises literally head and shoulders above the kids, they could greet many by name.

This stopped a lot of problems before they started, but most of the kids knew each other from school, or through sport and other interschool activities. Bernice and I concentrated on the girls' toilets and the exit doors. These doors had to be checked carefully, as kids being kids they would try to let in as many mates for free as they could. (The entry was $10, but this included all soft drink, the music and dancing.)

It was only after these underage nights had been running for a while that there was any trouble. When the kids were mostly from the North Shore, it was easy, but, as word spread, kids came from all over Sydney and with them came their problems. My daughter Kate was involved in an instance in the ladies' toilet where one group of girls were trying to bully others. Fortunately, she alerted Bernice and me, and we stopped the fracas, but not before one of the girls attending was frightened and upset, as described in this letter from her mother:

Please do not regard this as a letter of complaint. I am writing to advise you of a minor incident that occurred at your disco recently. I know you run a pretty "tight ship" and therefore would wish to be made aware of any problems. Last Friday night, a friend of my daughter's had a rather disturbing experience at your disco. She was confronted in the Ladies toilet by 15 girls demanding her clothes. Fortunately, five Aboriginal girls came to her rescue and she managed to leave the Ladies unscathed. My daughter and her friends assure me that you keep a constant eye on events at your disco and that your security staff are prompt at dealing with any likely behaviour.

As suggested by the mother, we took measures to increase security, both on the floor and at the front doors. The time had come when we had to police much more securely as word spread about the underage discos. To make the venue more secure, we employed two extra security guys at the front door whose only job was to use the metal detectors. One night we confiscated 12 knives and two knuckledusters. The kids carrying these were immediately handed over to the police outside, and word soon spread that this was not a place where trouble would be tolerated.

I do remember one boy who had to be refused entry every night. The first time he came, I thought he had the face of an angel and the manners of an old-time gent. Big brown eyes looked up at you; an expressive mouth smiled. He handed over his $10 and walked in. No trouble. An undercover policeman from the Graffiti Squad rushed up quickly.

"Lyn, that boy cannot come in. He is a violent, repeat juvenile offender." His looks did deceive, but didn't save him. I will say he was persistent though, but to no avail.

With the police outside—particularly the Graffiti Squad who alerted us to kids who could not be allowed entry—and the North Sydney Beat Police who lent a sobering presence, The Grizzies inside, the kids who reported if they thought there may be trouble, and the family and Bernice and Briony being alert, meant we were mostly free of trouble. However, there was another incident in the girls' toilet one night when two different nationalities thought they would come to blows, and another night when some boys of Lebanese and Aboriginal background thought they would have a fight. Both times the groups were put straight into the hands of the police. The upshot of this was deputations from various ethnic communities. They wanted these nights to continue for their youth and were asked if they could come and keep order. They did, and there was never any further trouble inside the premises.

But we did have one night of trouble outside when World War III erupted on Berry Street. This was about a year after the underage nights started. By this time, we had nationalities from all parts of Sydney turning up. No one knows how it started, but the whole street was suddenly alive with kids running and yelling. The street appeared to be wall-to-wall kids, from the corner of Mount Street to the corner of Walker Street. It was hard to tell what was happening or why. Police, security and family, we all rushed to stop what was happening. Aboriginal kids were around the corner in

Berry Lane. I rushed into the lane and gathered all the Aboriginal kids to get them inside. However, the two security guards—one man, one woman, both in their 60s—who had been employed to use the metal detectors as the youngsters entered each night, had rushed inside and locked the doors. Bad choice made there! And I haven't been able to live it down.

The police could not control the sudden eruption into violence of the many kids. Neither could our security, who had been locked outside. But these nights had been so popular with underage kids of all nationalities, that we again had deputations from the Greek, Aboriginal, Vietnamese and Lebanese communities. These guys wanted some of their senior people to be present each underage night so that there wouldn't be trouble.

"This is the only place our kids can come and they love it," we were told. "We want to make sure it continues for them."

Partly because of their presence and quick acting, there were no injuries or undue violence, just mayhem. In time, we realised that we had done enough: we had highlighted the need for safe places for underage teens.

A report in the *North Shore Times* on 2 February 1993, was the beginning of the end for us. It was headlined: "Color [sic] gangs under fire":

North Sydney police have called for reinforcements to deal with an influx of color gangs. Licensing Sergeant Ray Barry said the popularity of a disco for teenagers at McGettigan's nightclub on Fridays had attracted the gangs. Strict security meant there was no trouble inside the

Berry Street nightclub. "But the problem is the 100 to 150 kids who are not allowed into the disco and who congregate outside," Sgt Barry said. Sgt Barry said since the disco opened in September there had been an increase in petty crime around Berry St. He said the Graffiti Squad, Special Operations Group, Transit Police and North Sydney Beat Police would mount patrols in the area this month. "McGettigan's is doing a community service by getting local kids off the streets," Sgt Barry said. Nightclub owner Brian McGettigan said it was only a few who spoiled it for others.

Things calmed down, but after that night we decided our underage disco would have to end. By now, there were plenty of places operating underage nights and we turned it over to them. Many of these were started by community services, who were able to benefit from all we had learned and implemented. We were instrumental in telling them of our experiences: from metal detectors at the door to closely monitoring how long music with a heavy beat could play. One comment from a community meeting in South West Sydney in 1993 was: "The meeting was beneficial in providing us with invaluable information about how to set up and conduct an Under 18's Disco/Nightclub. We aim to establish a similar event at a local venue in the near future. Thank you both for your time, energy and inspiration."

McGettigan's was the first to introduce HSC Results parties. Attendees of these post-HSC parties came from surrounding schools: Monte Sant' Angelo, Loreto Kirribilli, St Aloysius'

College, Marist College North Shore, North Sydney Girls High School, St Joseph's Hunters Hill, and from much further afield.

Reported in the *Sydney Morning Herald* (date unknown) under the headline "Schoolgirls togged up for uniform celebration" were comments from SCEGGS student, who celebrated at McGettigan's first HSC Results party: "Yes, we've finished and we're going to have a big night. ... We're going to stay here until the club closes and then maybe go onto a party."

In the same article, McGettigan's manager Mark Richie said that the club had extended its hours to mark the special occasion The article finished: "While the students raged inside others were still queueing down the street in the hope of getting in to join in the fun. ... Thousands of other students hit the town with a vengeance last night to mark the end of the HSC. Even though much of the partying went on until the small hours today, police said there were no reports of trouble."

Controversy about McGettigan's over the four years we were running was varied, and can best be expressed in the letters we received. For McGettigan's *was* controversial. Not from the start, but as time progressed scuffles did break out. My mate Bernice took the bit between her teeth in 1992 when she replied to a letter from a headmistress of a well-known girls' school regarding end of year parties:

"I am aware of the activities my daughter participates in, both within the College and out of school hours. Your comments about the underage parties organised at such venues as McGettigan's are unwarranted and narrow-minded. I am sure you will agree that many of the problems surrounding the youth of today are caused by boredom and lack of supervised entertainment. My parental experience tells me that children/teenagers attending a function which is well-supervised is preferable to them roaming the streets, attempting to enter licensed premises, or attending private parties where there is no parental supervision, which is unfortunately becoming more prevalent in our society. Parents are encouraged to drop their children and collect them from these functions. They are invited onto the premises once they have arrived at the venue to collect their children and are invited to view the proceedings. Unfortunately, the information that has been circulated to parents via your letter is misleading and does not represent the opinions of all your staff and definitely not the opinions of parents of students from the College."

A contradictory, supportive letter was sent by the headmistress of another girls' school:

"This letter is to thank you for your assistance to raise money for our sporting body. So many of the students and the parents have told me of your generosity and your effort to ensure the success of the night, particularly by maintaining standards of supervision appropriate to the age group. That message has gone around our parent body too. With them, I am very grateful."

One of the parents attending the same function, wrote, in May 1992:

"I cannot thank you enough for your generosity, time and effort and facilities. It was a night to be remembered by all. ... Thank you also for your family's time and effort on 'the night'. They all worked so hard to make it such a fantastic night."

There are thank-you notes from many junior groups, mainly sporting clubs, where money was raised for the juniors. McGettigan's was much more than an underage disco, it performed a useful function in many ways for the community.

On 29 March 1993, the story of the underage disco went to air on the ABC's *7.30 Report* as part of a story on gang culture. A thank-you letter from Wendy Page, the story producer, was reaffirming to read: "One thing I learned from researching the story is that there is a terrible dearth of recreation places for so many teenagers in Sydney. It would be wonderful if there could be dozens of McGettigan's all over Sydney. No wonder your place attracts so many hundreds of people. Congratulations on running a fine operation."

The end of McGettigan's was the end of an era. These nights were an interesting experiment and provided somewhere safe for underage kids to go, but it was an experiment we were determined never to repeat. Nevertheless, McGettigan's holds great memories for many thousands of youngsters from all over Sydney and I am still astounded when I'm stopped by young adults who say, "We remember McGettigan's. It was great."

PART 5
PENRITH
1991–1996

Harley Was Not Me Darlin'

And in walked Harley. Long-striding, tall-standing, confident, swaggering Harley. Only trouble was, I didn't see him walking in, and I didn't see him standing!

It was 1991. McGettigan's had started and Brian was managing that hotel, so the responsibility for running Tattersall's Tavern fell on me. In fact, I felt as if I was running both hotels, and for a while I was.

Tatts had a fearsome reputation: it was the last beer before Emu Plains jail and the first beer when you got out. I didn't know this when we bought it. It was supposed to be a joint venture between me, Brian the Publican, Royce Simmons (super footballer), and Ron Willey (footy coach). Ron and Royce had some history behind them. At the time, Ron was the coach of the Penrith Panthers and the Australian Kangaroos, and had lived and coached in France and England. Royce was a star player and one-time captain of the Panthers. He was a Cowra boy who had moved there, married a lovely girl, Leanne, and they had a young family. Unfortunately, the deal to buy the tavern with Ron and Royce fell through, so we ended up buying it ourselves. When it came time to take it over, Brian the Publican said, "You wanted to buy this hotel, Lyn. You go and run it."

"I?" I replied indignantly. "It was nothing to do with me. The deal was between you three guys. Okay, I admit I looked at the figures. They were good, but my running it was definitely not part of the deal."

"You wanted it. You run it!" Logic wasn't one of Brian the Publican's strong points; neither was empathy. So when handover day came, out we went to Penrith. The tavern was signed over at midday and after buying the patrons drinks for about three hours, Brian the Publican was on his way, and the fun began.

This was a tavern, so we had to have food available during opening hours—even if it was only a pie or sandwich. At this point, this was all Tatts had. Brian the Publican's custom of shouting free drinks for the patrons on the opening a new venture—and having a few with them—rarely exists anymore as hotels are often run by companies and their managers rather than by a family. It was often the publican's wife they feared, especially if she was a tough, hard worker.

I was the "baddie", 153 cm, 58 kg and with a "no rot" attitude: barring (not allowing the offender back into the pub) was the order of the day if there was bad language, fighting or drugs. What did I walk into at Tatts? All three apparently, plus bar staff with a propensity for locking themselves in the office when trouble started. All except for Linda. She was a gem and could run a pub with a "no prisoners taken" attitude.

My modus operandi at any new pub was to take a swab (a cleaning cloth, usually cut from an old bar runner) in one hand, hang a small bucket over my arm (for emptying dirty ashtrays) and begin to clean the tables. That way I could get to meet the regulars and weigh them up. It was fun, as some customers thought I was a new staff member, which gave me an insight into their character before they realised who I was. The ones who knew I was the publican's wife generally had two opinions: (1) I was a hard worker, and (2) Brian the Publican was a lazy bugger.

Whatever. I was cleaning tables and chatting when Harley walked in with his obligatory blonde hanging off his arm. She was attractive. Harley could pull the good sorts. He was good-looking himself: 194cm, well-built, the Adonis of Penrith. He bought his girlfriend a drink and a schooner of squash for himself—Harley didn't drink, he didn't need to, as I was to find out later. They went to a table, pulled out a couple of chairs and sat down.

"Hello," I said amiably. Then I looked down. Harley had his feet up on one of my chairs.

"Take your feet off," I said. "What do you think you're doing dirtying my chair?"

Harley looked at me rather oddly, but got his feet off. There was a moment of silence around us, but then conversation started again. I didn't notice this overly much and alarm bells didn't start ringing. Things went along smoothly until about 11 p.m. By this time I had finished cleaning every table in the place, had spoken to every customer, and had been back and forth to the bar about 20 times. I had just turned to go back to the bar for the final time when I saw Harley standing behind the bar, schooner glass of squash in one hand, wet bar towel around his neck.

"What do you think you are doing?" I asked.

Harley said nothing. Just looked at me with his eyes wide open, eyebrows raised.

"Harley's just cool... cooling down," stuttered the bar attendant.

"I don't care what he's doing. He doesn't come behind my bar." As I said this, I reached out and took the schooner glass of squash from his hand. "Give me that towel," I demanded. Harley put the towel in my hand. "You're barred," I said. "Nobody comes into my bar, puts their feet on my chairs and then goes behind the bar."

Harley said nothing. He calmly walked out, collecting his blonde appendage on the way. I looked around to tell the barman to start closing up. There was no barman, but strangely enough there was a pickaxe handle on the bench at the back of the bar.

I wonder why that's there? I thought. Then, *I wonder where the barman is?* I went towards the side door to start the lock up. The barman appeared from the direction of the office.

"Where have you been?" I asked.

"I've been in the office," he said.

"Strange," I thought. "He's as white as a sheet."

For the next two weeks, I cleaned up the hotel. This meant barring unwanted customers (those who caused trouble for any reason) and arriving at 7 a.m. (before the staff arrived at 8 a.m.) to check if there were any new bullet holes in the windows. The hotel premises got a makeover—carpet shampooed, furniture repaired. The place started to look a lot better and the atmosphere had improved. Good, I thought, this place will be okay.

Then in walked Harley—tall, good-looking Harley with a new appendage on his arm. This time I was serving behind the bar. Suddenly the barman (the same one) bolted to the office. *Strange,* I thought. I looked up to see Harley seated at a table with an attractive bird. *What is he doing here?* I thought. *He's barred. He's staying barred!* With that, I walked around the bar towards Harley. He looked up, saw me, and he and his girlfriend decided to leave. *That's good,* I thought. *I don't need another confrontation today.*

Suddenly the barman appeared, again from the direction of the office. Again he looked green.

"What happened to you this time?" I asked. "You seem to disappear at the oddest times."

"I wasn't feeling well," he said, "so I ducked out the back to take a couple of aspirin."

It sounded a bit contrived.

After two weeks of managing Tatts and driving to and from Sydney city daily, I thought I would head home and let Brian the Publican manage for a while.

"Look Brian," I said, "it's time you took over for a while. I'd like to spend some time at home with the kids."

"Okay," he replied kindly. So that Saturday night after closing at 10 p.m., I went out into the laneway and got into my 1969 white VW. I remember it was pouring down rain and it took a long time to get home to Mosman. Next morning, Brian the Publican got into his Holden Statesman and drove to Penrith to be ready to open at 10 a.m. All went smoothly for him that day. He drove home that night thinking that it was an easy place to run and was looking

171

forward to the nights during the week when Ron Willey, Royce, Peter Kelly, "Penguin" and the Panthers team would come in after training for a few beers. Monday went by okay. Tuesday came. I got a phone call about 9 p.m.

"Did you bar Harley?"

"Of course I barred him. He had his feet on my chairs, he went behind the bar where he shouldn't have been. Put him out! He's never to be in Tatts again!"

"I'm not barring him," shouted Brian. "Do you know who he is? He's a body builder, a fitness freak and he's on steroids. He's 190cm. He's a man mountain. Do you know what he does for a living? He's a stand-over man. If you don't understand that, let me tell you—he bashes people for a living."

"I don't care who he is," I replied. "He's barred. You put him out."

"I'm not putting him out," repeated Brian the Publican. "I don't want to be the first astronaut going around Australia after one of his hits!"

He didn't bar him. "Brian-y" and Harley got on quite well. Harley kept an eye on the pub and kept out unsavoury characters on Brian's watch. Brian-y helped him out when he needed a few bob. However, Harley never appeared when I was there. In those days, I think women had a distinct advantage over men when dealing with difficult male customers. For some reason women were respected, maybe because we were basically fearless, didn't swear, and all the customers knew that we were hard workers. Many did as I did: worked in the bars, did the books (bookkeeping) for the hotel, hired and fired staff, all the while looking after their families. Sometimes, when watching a Wild West movie and seeing the tough woman who runs the saloon, I am reminded of the female publicans of the '60s, '70s and '80s. Mind you, we mostly looked, dressed and spoke like Sybil Fawlty—beautifully clothed, with short blonde hair that seemed to be coiffed once a week.

The situation with Harley went on for about another six months. He was in when Brian-y was there, out when Lynnie was there. Then one day Brian-y rang me.

"Guess what has happened? Harley has been arrested. He was given a contract on someone at Newtown. He slit someone's throat and put three holes in their head to make sure they were dead. I knew he was mad, but I didn't think that he was that bloody mad! He's in jail, never to be released."

To this day, I wonder why Harley didn't come into the pub when I was working. Perhaps he just couldn't be bothered? Loss of reputation? Or perhaps it was respect for "the little woman"?

Paddy the Pusher

Another "person of interest" at Tatts in the early '90s was Paddy the Irishman. By this time I'd stopped full-time work at Penrith but we still had McGettigan's. Tatts Tavern needed a full-time manager. When Brian was at Penshurst, a customer, a part-time real estate valuer, Ernie, talked to him about learning the hotel game and eventually buying one of his own. Brian trained him up in the hotel business at Penshurst, and then Ernie went on to successfully run his own hotels. When we asked him to come to Penrith to run it, and have a share in it, Ernie agreed as long as we bought him a house, which we did in the Penrith suburb of Mount Pleasant. Ernie knew what he was doing, got on well with staff and regulars, and ran a good ship.

On his days off, Brian the Publican or I went to take over. Linda the super-manager was there to back me up if there was any trouble.

One Tuesday she came over and said, "Lyn, see that ginger-haired bloke over there at the TAB? He's just out of jail. He's been barred by Ernie."

"Okay," I said, "I'll go and put him out." So over I went and fronted Paddy.

"What are you doing in here having a bet? Ernie barred you."

"Ernie didn't bar me," Paddy replied. "He said I could come in."

"Don't lie to me," I said as I looked over the top of his curly-haired ginger head, and then down to the teardrop tattoo under his left eye. "Come over here and we'll have a chat." So over we went to the corner of the tavern. We were on a level playing field—both about the same height. Soon words, looks, but no fists were flying around. Paddy had kissed the Blarney Stone. His stories and excuses would have been rich fodder for any TV series.

"Enough of the blarney, Paddy. I'm telling you how it will be. I'll let you in to have a bet. You can have one schooner while you're here. Any trouble and you're out. You will never be allowed back in."

"Okay," he said, and a deal was struck that lasted for as long as he came in. Paddy came in, regular as clockwork, had his bet, had his schooner, caused no trouble. Until one day I realised that I hadn't seen him for a while. I asked Linda.

"No," she said with a funny look. "He hasn't been in for three weeks."

Odd, I thought. *He's probably back in jail.*

I didn't give his absence any more thought until one of the regulars said, "I believe you were asking after Paddy, Lyn."

"Yes," I replied. "Where is the little Irishman?"

"I'm not telling you this," he said. "You didn't hear it from me, but Paddy's dead. He thought he'd get into the drug game big time, so one night he and his mates cornered Billy the Bull and explained to him nicely that they were taking over his drug territory. Billy was not impressed and exploded. He started bellowing and lashed out, but Paddy's boys knocked him to the ground and held him there. Paddy put the boot in, but he overdid it a bit. Too many kicks to the head and chest, we reckon. They left Billy there beside the park unconscious, and cleared off, thinking they were safe. When a passer-by found him, it was too late. I heard on the grapevine that his heart had stopped."

"How long did Paddy survive as 'King of the Drug Trade' ? I asked.

"A couple of days," he replied. "I'm not saying who got to him, but word has it that he was weighed down and thrown in the Nepean."

Poor, stupid idiot, I thought. He really was pretty harmless.

A week later, two uniform cops called into the tavern and asked to see me in the office. Unusual, I thought, usually the cops just walk in early in the morning, ask if there are any problems and leave.

"Hello guys," I said. "How can I help you?"

"Have you seen Paddy the Irishman?" asked the overweight sergeant.

"No," I said, "not for about a month. Why do you want to find him?" I asked.

"Do you know where we can find him?" Sarge repeated.

"Well," I replied. "I'm not telling you this, but I don't think he'll be around Penrith for a while. The word around town is that he took part in the killing of Billy the Bull. The word around town is that he won't be found until the Penrith River floods. I heard he's somewhere in there and very unlikely to float to the top anytime soon."

"How do you know?" asked the Sarge as his skinny young offsider busily scribbled in his notebook. (In those days, they had what I considered was a good policing system—a young cop was paired with an older, experienced one. It seemed to work well as the older man shared his experience and knowledge of police work with the younger one.)

"Well, I don't really know," I replied. "It's just something I heard on the grapevine." That was all I was prepared to say and I left it at that. After all, they now knew as much as me. By this time, I figured all those in Penrith who needed to know, would know. The two cops left.

To this day, Paddy has never been found. I don't think the Penrith River has flooded since then.

The Publican and The Prostitute

I walked into the Tatts Tavern after two weeks' holiday with the family, to relieve the manager, Linda. I was greeted with heartfelt sighs from the two old guys who habitually occupied the bar stools closest to the door.

"Thank heavens you're back, Lyn," they said. "You're not going to be happy about what's going on."

"What do you mean? What is going on?" I demanded.

One of them, Ted, looked at his watch, looked over to his mate, Harry, nodded and said, "Only 10 minutes to wait, eh Harry?"

Harry sipped his middy, nodded and commented, "Twelve o'clock on the knocker. She should be coming through the door behind us."

By this time I was losing patience. "Who will be coming through?" I asked. "You'd better hurry up and tell me!"

"The prostitute," said Ted.

Harry nodded sagely.

"What prostitute?" I asked.

"Well," continued Ted, "she comes in here every Friday and sets herself up in the first cubicle in the men's toilet. The guys line up outside and take their turn."

"What!" I exploded. "That will be stopped right now!" I looked for the manager to get some kind of explanation. No manager visible and the time was high noon!

The door to the public bar swung open. In swayed a dark-haired woman, doped out of her mind, precariously balancing on red high heels and simultaneously managing to drag off her gold lamé cardigan and sling her handbag to the skinny, grubby pimp following her. She swayed again and started sashaying towards the queue that had magically formed outside the men's toilet. The men leered. I was galvanised into action.

"What do you think you're doing?" I yelled as I grabbed the pimp and swung him around. "Get her and yourself out of here."

"You can't do that," he whimpered as he hit the doorway.

"Watch me!" I said. I stalked over and grabbed her. Not so easy. She was much heavier and by this time was very precariously teetering.

"You can't do this," she mumbled as she tried to focus on me.

"Watch me!" I repeated. Seemed to be the day for repetition. She very quickly followed the pimp through the same doorway, and none too gently! The queue of waiting men disappeared as if by magic. There was no repeat business from her or her customers. I had never seen any of them before, and I didn't again.

A Hospital Case

It was 1993. Brian the Publican was ill. He had been diagnosed with a bad heart and was in hospital where one of the surgeons who thought that he was the best—The Trump—was Brian's doctor. The Trump attempted to put in a stent. Brian the Publican's father had also had a bad heart and he had died on the operating table whilst having heart surgery, so Brian was paranoid the same thing would happen to him. I spoke to The Trump on two occasions about my husband's fear, but The Trump did not appear too concerned. In desperation, I decided to ring and speak to his secretary.

"Brian is afraid he is going to die on the operating table as his father did. Please tell the doctor to approach him carefully and explain to him what he is about to do." I could have saved my 10-cent phone call for all the good it did. Advice disregarded.

On operating day The Trump approached the Publican, who was lying on the operating table, deceptively calm, deceptively sedated. Brian saw The Trump approaching with what appeared to be a knife in his hand. With great native cunning, Brian allowed The Trump to draw near. Now, Brian the Publican had been a great Union player in his day and was one of the all-time sporting greats produced by St Joseph's College, Hunters Hill. With an almighty heave, Brian rose up from the table and grabbed the Trump around the throat. Perhaps he was reliving his Joey's vs. Riverview matches! Mayhem! Nurses and theatre staff materialised beside the bed and grabbed Brian. Someone managed to sedate him.

I arrived at the hospital at noon, about two hours after his operation. I expected that Brian would be up from recovery. Not so. Two p.m. came and went.

"We have had some unexpected developments down in the theatre," said the ward sister, answering my enquiry. "Nothing to worry about. He'll be up soon."

Four p.m.

"Are you sure everything is all right?" I had begun to worry.

"Absolutely all right," she said as she hastened away.

Six p.m. Same conversation but the hastening seemed a bit more hastened.

Then at 8 p.m., Brian finally materialised through the lift doors. However, he still appeared to be largely out of it. *That's strange,* I thought. *He shouldn't be still out of it.* Later I found out what had happened. In the panic, Brian had been sedated too heavily. Things went downhill from there at a rapid rate.

The following day when I visited him at 2 p.m., he was in an isolation room outside the nurses' station. Tubes were coming out of him, monitors were beeping, a fan was whirring and a wet sheet had been draped over him. He appeared to be in a bad way with an extremely high temperature.

"I'm dying," he managed to croak (as all men do!) before he

closed his eyes again and went to sleep. I thought I had better phone around and let his family know what was happening. The first person to arrive that afternoon was his sister, Leonie. One look at him and she was also convinced that he was dying! The next day she arrived with her three children, Catherine, Margaret-Mary and Bill, to say goodbye to their uncle before he died. Before leaving the hospital, she told me to go home and cook him some poached fresh peaches. "He loves those," she said. "Make sure you cook fresh ones and don't give him those tinned ones!" It sounded like the last meal on San Quentin death row.

The next person to arrive was my mate Bernice. Bernice arrived with five children in tow: my three, her two, and The Boiler, Mrs Lewis. (Mrs Lewis was called The Boiler by us, with great affection, but Mrs Lewis by the children.) We didn't tell the kids the dire news but gave them a pile of lollies and chocolates so that they could sit in his room and eat them. We figured lollies would serve two purposes: fool the kids and keep them quiet! They did and the five kids happily went home with Mrs Lewis to do their homework. The nursing staff thought she was Brian the Publican's mother! Grandmother taking the grandchildren home.

The next to arrive with an appropriately serious look on his face, was his cousin Bernie. His entry to the "death room" (even though Brian the Publican was now compos mentis) was dramatic. He tripped over one of the tubes connected to a monitoring machine and all hell broke loose, not to mention the dripping blood! Nurses came running, visitors were evacuated. Visitors were then restricted to one at a time, family only! Bernice was still there morally supporting me throughout this tragic time, and when 9 p.m. came we thought we had better leave and do something more useful. There was no point in staying—Brian was sedated again, the kids were okay, and we thought that we might have a funeral to plan. What better place to plan it than in a pub over a few drinks? So we adjourned to the closest hotel to the hospital, where we found this complex matter took until 1 a.m. to sort out. Somehow one of us drove home to Mosman to find all the kids and Mrs Lewis asleep. We decided that we had done enough and should go to sleep too. Tomorrow could be a big day.

Tomorrow was, but not à la funeral! There were no tears and no undertakers. Luckily, Brian the Publican was as well as a man with golden staph could be, for apparently that was what he had caught. In the furore in the theatre when the stent was to be inserted, it was thought that a hand had inadvertently entered Brian's wound. When Bernice and I arrived, we were allowed to visit for a few minutes and then adjourned to the waiting room until the nurses had finished their checks. As we were sitting there, two senior police from North Sydney station turned up in uniforms and caps. Caps worn! It was a bit of a joke to the public in those days that if the police wore their caps, things were serious!

"Hello Lyn. We've come to pay our respects to Brian. We hear he's not in a good way." In they went. Five minutes later out came two nurses and a sister.

"Do you mind if we ask you something?' the sister asked.

"Not at all," I replied, thinking it was something to do with Brian's health. "I'll help you in any way I can."

"Well," said the sister, "is your husband a criminal?"

"No," I replied, laughing despite the seriousness. "He's a publican and the two police with him are friends from North Sydney Police Station." Relief visible on their faces, they happily went back to tend to the sick man. A few seconds later there was a look of consternation on my face.

"Oh, no!" I said to Bernice, pointing to the doorway. "Look who's here now!"

"Who?" she said. "Oh, those two painters. What's wrong with them? I've never seen them before."

"No, you wouldn't have," I said. "They're from Tatts at Penrith, and they're not painters. They're criminals. I wonder why they are disguised?" All I could think was that they were outside their own territory or had perhaps pulled a job nearby.

Bernice didn't look convinced. They were caricatures. Another pair looking like Laurel and Hardy, only they weren't there to rob us. *Must be a crook's favourite disguise,* I thought. The fat one had paint-splattered overalls straining across his stomach; the skinny one had his even more paint-splattered ones hanging off his scrawny frame. Both wore baseball caps pulled low over their foreheads, and even these were paint-splattered.

"Hello, Lyn," said Laurel, peering down under the bill of his cap. "I hear the old man's dying."

"Yeah," echoed the skinny sidekick. "The old man's dying."

"Well," I said, "he's not, but you'd better not go in there now. There are two cops visiting him. They've been in there ten minutes already and should be due to come out."

"Shit!" said Laurel.

"Shit!" echoed Hardy.

"Be back in ten minutes," said Laurel.

"Back in ten," echoed Hardy as they both sprinted for the door. Just at that moment, the cops appeared back in the waiting room.

"Doesn't look good, Lyn, but they assure us that he will pull through."

"Thanks guys, and thanks for coming," I said as I hurried them to the lift, hoping they wouldn't run into Brian's other two visitors as they left. The down lift doors closed. I breathed a sigh of relief. Then the up-lift doors opened. Laurel and Hardy stepped out. They visited the sick room and came out shaking their heads.

"Now look, Lyn," said Laurel seriously, "I want to have a talk to you. Things look bad in there. We'll be burying him soon, but I don't want you to worry. We'll look after you. The whole pub's behind you—funeral expenses, wake, all taken care of. Then, the plan is this. I'll marry you and we can set up a brothel. There's a vacant floor above the tavern. It's a good business: better takings, easier work than a pub, but you can keep running that, too, if you want to. All you have to do is mind the books and I'll do the heavy work. There won't be any trouble."

"Thanks very much," I said, "but I don't think I can marry you while he's still alive, and I think he'll pull through."

"The offer's there, Lyn. We respect you out Penrith way and will see you right."

I wondered what they offered if they *don't* respect you? I began praying fervently for Brian's recovery.

185

Brian recovered enough to be transferred to St Vincent's Hospital in Darlinghurst, thanks to Col Joye and his neighbour Professor Michael O'Rourke, who kindly took him on as a patient. Brian's reputation preceded him. All of St Vincent's knew what had happened at the previous hospital and I do believe he was the star of a skit at the St Vincent's Christmas pantomime. As one doctor put it, as Brian was being wheeled down to the theatre at St Vincent's: "Brian, I know what happened at the other hospital. I'll have the prettiest nurses in the theatre. You just have to do what they tell you and keep your hands behind your back. If I see your hands at your sides, I will knock you out!"

This doctor was over 183cm, had played rugby and was more than capable of knocking Brian out. It was a miracle that Brian's heart condition was treated just with medication at St. Vincent's. We as a family have had a great devotion to Saint Mary MacKillop. Whatever the medical reason for less invasive treatment, we put it down to a miracle. Often Mary's miracles occur when a doctor is changed. In this case, both the doctor and the hospital had been changed. Twenty-five years on, Brian is still alive and telling pub stories.

I Don't Understand It

I enjoyed Penrith. It was my favourite pub. And it appeared that Penrith liked and respected me. But this fact, and how much, was not made clear to me until many years later.

My two old men in beige sweaters, beige golf shirts, beige trousers and brown slip-on shoes who always drank quietly at the bar, downing their schooners of Resch's in a methodical fashion, are the integral part of this puzzle. "Hello Lyn," they would quietly greet me each morning as I walked in. One morning in the first two weeks, after they had watched me clean up the hotel, they called me over, shook my hand and told me that I would be looked after for the rest of my life. I didn't realise the significance of this until many years later.

The looking-after took effect immediately. Being conscientious, I did what the police recommended re safety and security in and around the hotel. I went to the bank at a different time each day, took different routes there, and even carried different bags. In those days, banking was done on a daily basis and the publican usually did it him or herself. The days of a security company collecting your cash had not arrived.

"Hi Lyn. Nice day isn't it?" called out a cheery character who appeared to be selling hot goods out of the boot of his car, which was parked across the road from the police station.

"Hi," I waved back. "Beautiful." Never seen him before in my life. That he knew my name didn't gel, as a lot of people knew you when you were in the pub game, but you didn't necessarily remember them or their name, or when you had met them.

This was my first day of protection at Penrith. This sort of thing happened every day as I was out and about. Thinking back, robberies at the premises stopped. After the first two weeks of getting in early—to check for fresh bullet holes in the windows, or to see if anyone was hiding in the toilets or office to try and force me to open the safe—I was able to relax. You usually had an inkling if someone was inside. Tatts closed at 10 p.m. or midnight, and the toilets were checked, always by two staff, to see if any patrons had stayed behind—their intention had to be robbery as all alcohol was taken off the shelves and locked away. All clear. Then the night staff left.

Before opening the side door in the early morning, I checked to see if there were any jemmy marks—this indicated forced entry and that perpetrators could be inside. If so, I went to the nearest outside phone and rang the police. No mobiles then. It was important you did this for insurance purposes: no forced entry, not so easy to claim compensation. Often robbery was an inside job, and this involved a little more paperwork. There were publicans who had been locked in their cellars, in their walk-in safes and even one who had been locked in his cool room (in this case, the thoughtful thieves had turned off the power so he didn't get unnecessarily cold).

My life was more protected than the publican who was locked in the cold.

Many years later, I saw two young Penrith patrons wandering through the Kincumber pub beer garden.

"Hello boys," I exclaimed happily. "What are you doing here? It's good to see you. Come in and I'll buy you a schooner."

"You haven't seen us, Lyn."

"What do you mean I haven't seen you? I'm talking to you."

"You haven't seen us," they repeated. "Every few months for the rest of your life someone will check on you and make sure that you are okay. You will never see them."

"Okay." I didn't ask any questions. "Thanks guys."

They left. I walked inside. I didn't have a clue why this was happening, only that it was connected to the gentlemanly old guys in their beige clothes who sat at the bar so quietly. Then, in 2014, it happened again. This was 20 years after Penrith, so I assumed that the invisible protection had been happening all this time.

I was living in Kirribilli by this time. I was getting on the train at Milsons Point to go to the city for a yoga class when I noticed a short, red-haired, red-bearded man detach himself from the wall outside the station and get onto the same train as me, but in the next carriage. My powers of observation aren't that good, but after years of being aware of who and what was around me, I suppose I registered him in my subconscious. Oddly, he was outside the gym when I came out and even more oddly, he got onto the same train and got off at the same station. No alarm bells. Nothing registered. I happily wandered home, daily paper under my arm, takeaway coffee in my hand.

The next three days were yoga days. Same thing. But he went no further than Town Hall station and was there to catch the same train home as I did. Still no alarm bells ringing. Then, on the fifth day, the same routine.

"I suppose I'll have to have a word with the police if this keeps up."

But this didn't keep up. I never saw him again.

Who were those two fatherly figures who gave me protection in Penrith? Why was their influence still so strong after so many years? I don't doubt that it continues and will continue long after their deaths and until mine.

Thank you, guys.

A Tree Change

After eight eventful years at Penrith, we decided to sell the tavern. We had built it into a successful business and it had lost its reputation as a "bloodbath" many years previously. It had seen its share of footballers pass through its doors for a drink after training, and some called in for business reasons. Most memorable of these were the Mortimer boys. They had a business putting shuffleboard tables into premises. Coloured discs were pushed around the shuffleboard table to score points. The money put into these operated on the same basis as a pinball game. A percentage went to the hotel and the rest to the owner of the game. Cigarette machines operated the same way. There was big money in these machines for the tobacco companies, and thus fierce competition to get them onto your premises.

There was one game that would leave today's generation aghast. This was The Great Crab Race Tournament. This game ensured huge crowds of punters and drinkers. The organiser would come in with his table and his ten crabs. The crabs were humanely kept in a box lined with damp hessian. "After all, mate," he would say as he downed his first schooner, "I look after them. They're valuable."

The large table was set up in the middle of the bar. It had ten lanes painted on it. There was a start and finish line. Now, you would be forgiven for wondering how the crab knew to stick to its lane. Easy. The crab had a corresponding number painted on it. It didn't matter if it wandered into another lane. The book had been set. The odds were known.

Betting started. The blokes placed their money over the finish line. It said a lot for the punters that there was never a fight or a disagreement over whose money it was. When the race was run, the organiser's offsider would gather up the money and pay the winners. There were usually only five races. After all, the boys had to get to work the next day. The organiser was happy, the punters were happy, and the pub owner was ecstatic (usually a big bar-taking night or afternoon). The government wasn't: punting money it didn't get a share in. Another case for legalised gaming via the TAB.

All this fun aside, it was time to go. Our 10 years that we normally spent in one pub was nearly up. No reason for this 10-year syndrome other than the pub had been built up enough to sell at a profit. Our time of departure was precipitated by Ernie the manager's illness. Unfortunately, he got an infected tooth. The infection travelled throughout his body and affected his heart. He was on medication, but for some reason did not take some of this medication, with dire consequences. He was rushed to Penrith Hospital but passed away soon after.

We sold Penrith and concentrated on Jindabyne.

I remember Penrith with great affection. It was my favourite pub, possibly for the characters and the element of surprise that was always waiting. There was usually some drama, particularly in the early days, but even when it was "respectable" it was always interesting.

PART 6
JINDABYNE
1989–1998

A Bit of Gumption

In 1989, we bought the Lake Jindabyne Hotel. It was just before Paul Keating's "recession that (we) had to have" and it did take its toll when interest rates rose to 19 per cent, which many commercial borrowers had to pay. This recession wasn't on our mind when we bought the hotel.

Hotel auctions were conducted in Bridge Street, Sydney. The auction rooms were much the same as any auction. Spotters stood around the sides; the buyers, mostly publicans, sat in the middle on rows of seats. Some were there to buy, some merely to look. It was always pretty subdued. Publicans are a secretive breed—all information is kept close to their chests. After greeting each other and exchanging gossip, they took their seats. Gossip is always rife and exaggerated in the insular hotel world. In those days, it was always helped along by the nature of publicans, a "hail fellow well met" breed who were an active presence in their hotels, so they knew who was doing what and with whom.

This day was no different. Brian the Publican, Kevin the Accountant and I had turned up to buy a hotel. We had looked through the trading figures of four hotels, and three held up. Two of these hotels were up for bids but each time Kevin the

Accountant said, "Too expensive." By the time the Lake Jindabyne came up, I was out of patience with both of them.

"Show a bit of gumption," I goaded. "For heaven's sake, buy one!"

We bought Lake Jindabyne Hotel.

Showdown at the LJH

The red-brick hotel and motel sprawled along the shores of the lake and it was the first thing you saw as you drove into town.

"Welcome to the Lake Jindabyne Hotel" proclaimed the chalet-inspired sign at the front driveway. The whole thing, including the grounds fronting the lake and the carparks, was a huge complex. In winter the 40-room motel, with bunk beds installed in the large rooms, could sleep up to 200 people. The lower level of the hotel had a pool, a spa and sauna, a gym, and a Thai restaurant. The ground level had an Australian bistro, an entertainment room that could hold a thousand people on big-band nights, an equally large public bar and a bottle shop. And we did have some big bands perform there: Hunters and Collectors, Midnight Oil, Silverchair, Powderfinger, Yothu Yindi, Hoodoo Gurus, Divinyls, 1927, Grinspoon, Chocolate Starfish, Screaming Jets—as well as name performers—Angry Anderson, Kate Ceberano, Marcia Hines, Paul Kelly, Lee Kernaghan.

What we didn't foresee was that with Jindabyne would come the tyranny of distance. It was a five-and-a-half-hour drive from Sydney. Brian the Publican and I would go down monthly for a three-day visit. We would check the books, talk to the managers, have a few drinks with the locals, and then leave on the third day to get back to Sydney.

"They will be glad to see you go and be out waving you goodbye," said my father Jack, "and by the time you cross the bridge over the Snowy River towards Cooma, they'll all be back to their own ways." How right he was. "Out of sight, out of mind" is another adage that comes to mind, and was probably on the minds of the staff!

After about two months I got the feeling something was not altogether right at Jindabyne. The weekly figures were good, but the wage percentage was too high. Normal wage-to-takings percentage we tried to keep at 10 per cent, but these were running at 18 per cent. It was summer and this was an extremely quiet trading time. It was necessary, but hard, to keep wages as low as possible. Our husband-and-wife management team was very good, but did not seem to be able to find any more corners to cut.

"I don't think things are right down there," I said to Brian the Publican. "I'll get on the 1 p.m. plane tomorrow and get down there. I won't tell anyone that I'm coming. It will be a surprise visit."

"Okay," agreed Brian the Publican.

At 3 p.m. on Tuesday afternoon I arrived at the pub. I walked into the office to the great surprise of the very attractive receptionist, Suzie.

"Hello Suzie," I said. "How are you?"

"Oh. Hi, Lyn. I'm fine. We didn't expect you."

"I just decided to come down and see how things are going.

There are a few things I want to clear up. Call a staff meeting of all staff for 10 a.m. tomorrow morning. The duration of the meeting will be about two hours. All staff will be paid for attending. Any staff that don't attend won't have a job."

Suzie looked at me. Suzie said nothing. Suzie started making phone calls. With a staff of approximately 50 at this time, it took her a while. Meanwhile, I spoke to the managers, checked the figures, had dinner, had a few drinks, and went to bed.

The next morning I dressed in a red power suit, complete with high heels, and went up to the room where we were to meet. Earlier I had checked it was set up the way I had wanted it—rows of chairs, top table, side table—ready for the papers I had brought with me.

The staff, including the manager, were there waiting, chattering, laughing and generally enjoying their paid-for holiday, some swinging their legs nonchalantly.

This says a lot about the situation here, I thought as I surveyed the configurations of the groups gathered, the sense of ease and relaxed messages of their body language.

"Thank you for coming," I began. "You are all now sacked. I will explain to you what a work contract is and those of you who choose to work under these conditions will be re-employed. In brief, it means a fair day's work for a fair day's pay. I do not rob anyone. You will be paid for everything to which you are entitled. Any grievances or any suggestions for improvement to working routines will be listened to. My door is always open.

"If you have a problem with a fellow staff member, then I

prefer you settle it between yourselves. If you cannot resolve the matter, then you can both come to see me and discuss the problem. As I get to know the staff and their work ethics, supervisors will be appointed at an increased rate of pay. These supervisors should make the step of coming to see me a last resort. To make the grievance procedure easier, directives will be implemented, such as a bar opening/closing procedure, which will take care of many grievances that generally involve the outgoing staff not leaving the bar as clean as they would wish to find it when they start work. Other procedures, and staff appearance and attitude will be outlined in the manual, which will be given to each staff member who chooses to stay.

"In conclusion, and before answering any questions you may have, I would like you all to know that closing time means closing time; staff drinks means two per staff member—wine, beer or bottom-shelf spirit*; members of the public, police, friends and staff who were on an earlier shift do not stay behind after closing time. (*Bottom-shelf spirits are sometimes called "house pours" and are generally a cheaper generic brand rather than a proprietary brand such as Tia Maria or Jim Beam.)

"Also, the practice of leaving the three end motel rooms made up, and the back window open, for patrons who have had a few too many and want to sleep it off, is over."

Open mouths stared at me. There was not one sound. Then gradually, the atmosphere changed. Silence gave way to angry babble.

"Who does she think she is? Walking in here and telling us what to do? She has her own and Buckley's."

They will find out, I thought, as I prepared for the barrage of questions. Mostly they were along the lines of statements like "we won't change". One-and-a-half hours later, I again reiterated that the staff who chose to remain could see the new work conditions, which would also be read out and discussed. Another one-and-a-half hours later, most faces looked relieved, if not happy. The conditions were not onerous. The one that caused the most angst was that staff were to turn up ten minutes before the start of their appointed shift time so they could communicate with the outgoing staff re cleaning to be completed and any customers that might cause a problem if they were still in the bar in an hour's time. However, we managed to get over that one.

All the staff signed their "Conditions of Work" and took their handbooks. All, that is, except three.

"We're not doing this," the spokeswoman Julie said. "We are going to resign."

"I'm sorry to hear that," I said. "I'll have your pay made up now and you can collect it from the office."

As the room emptied, I realised that I had plenty of time for my 3.30 p.m. return flight from Cooma to Sydney. I thought I would go to Cooma airport early and have a quiet and peaceful drink at Maggie's Bar. It was a good thing I did.

If I had stayed in Jindabyne, I would have witnessed a showdown. But it was not at the O.K. Corral. It was at the pub. Apparently, the three disgruntled staff had arrived home and told their husbands about the meeting. The husbands were outraged. They decided to ride into town Jindabyne-style: three of them in a brown, dusty ute, rattling along the corrugated dirt roads, grasping their shotguns in their hands. They arrived at the LJH, only to find that their quarry had left.

I wonder what they would have done if I had still been there?

Once the parameters had been laid out so clearly, everyone knew where they stood, and things did improve. The wage bill was lower now the manager was rostering the staff more efficiently. Instead of work that had to be done at Saturday's penalty rates, it was completed on Friday before knocking off. No one slept off Friday night's or Saturday's hangover in the rooms anymore, so that decreased the housemaid bill.

The chemicals bill also went down. Cheryl, the housekeeper, was an absolute gem and rostered firmly but fairly. She meted out cleaning chemicals to the bars, the hotel cleaners and the motel staff, and kept an accurate record of what, when and where any product was used. This meant a big saving.

Staff rostering in the bars was tightened up. Drinks ceased to be given away to mates, the two staff drinks rule was not abused, the hangers-on disappeared (at least when the staff knew I was on the premises), and all waste drinks, that is, those that had been poured by mistake, were recorded. So the bar percentages went up, profitability increased and the accountant was happy.

After this, I didn't think I would make too many friends amongst the LJH staff, but I did have their respect.

As Jindabyne was seasonal, I took a very active role over the slower summer period. Interest rates were 19%, so the only way to keep the bank at bay was to work hard yourself, usually from 5 a.m.

when I would get up to prepare breakfast for the motel guests, clean the rooms with Cheryl the Housekeeper, then man the office until 9 p.m. It was definitely not always an easy life.

The Snow Ball

Not all dramatic events associated with my life happened within the Jindabyne Hotel. Often there were outside events, but connected to the hotel like beer lines are to kegs. This super-dramatic event happened in Jindabyne at the bowling club. The McGettigan family—Brian the Publican, Kate our daughter and her partner, Debbie, and, of course, myself—had only been in Jindabyne about a year, but already my reputation was not that of a kind-hearted, "have a drink on me" kind of person. It was more "She's a bitch." You win some, you lose some.

The Snow Ball was held every year before the start of the skiing season and was the big social event of the year. It was held to raise money for the community, and this year, money was being raised for the public walkway around the lake. There was always a theme. This year's theme was "Outer Space". Consequently, our group were all dressed as people from another planet. I was dressed entirely in silver: wig, cloak, jumpsuit and high-heeled, pointy-toed stilettos. The stilettos are an important detail!

We were standing at the bar. We being Brian the Publican and I, and our guests, ex-boxer David and his wife, Janis; Ruth and Earl from the bush town of Dunedoo; Barbara and Peter Joseph;

Col Joye and Dalys; and two jockeys from Sydney and their wives. It was a happy group and got happier as the consumption of beer and rum and coke increased. These drinks were the traditional aperitifs to the sit-down dinner, accompanied by more drinks, of course, big-band entertainment and dancing.

All the town and surrounding districts had turned up, about 500 people—one of these being "The Breach", nicknamed Breachey, probably because when he saw an opening, he rushed right in. Probably his breach tonight was one of the code of conduct variety. Breachey was one of the town's characters. He was only about 26 at the time, skinny, yellow teeth, and habitually wore cowboy boots and jeans. He had what looked like a scar across his throat. Gossip had it that he had the unfortunate habit of cutting his throat about once a year, usually before Christmas. However, it was never deep enough to kill him! I never believed this. Gossip can run wild and the smallest thing can assume huge proportions.

On this night I can only assume that Breachey had developed a dislike of me. I don't think to this day he or I know the reason for it. Perhaps Bundy OP had something to do with it.

The group was relaxed. Conversation was entertaining but repetitive, as it is after quite a few drinks.

Suddenly Breachey fronted me.

"I'm going to kill you," he said.

I remembered what my father Jack had advised me: "Always say 'You had better make sure', otherwise I'll finish it."

So I took Jack's advice and quoted his famous line. It had no effect on Breachey. I doubt if he even heard it. He bared his teeth, definitely yellow, and backed towards the rear wall of the bar to get a run up. Unfortunately, the section of the back wall that he chose was a doorway leading to downstairs. Breachey disappeared. The last thing I saw was the heels of his cowboy boots as he tumbled backwards.

"That's the end of him," I said as I leant one elbow on the bar, one silver-stilettoed foot up on the rail around the bar, glass of red wine held in the other hand.

"Thank God, Lyn," said David the ex-boxer. "I couldn't help you, you know. My hands are registered weapons."

"That's right," echoed his wife. "He'll go to jail if he gets into a fight."

"Thank God," echoed the two small jockeys as their wives nodded. "He would have made mincemeat of us!"

Suddenly, our complacency was shattered. The door was flung back against the wall and Breachey erupted in, unscathed and breathing fire. He rushed at me, hands clenched into fists. I swear he was frothing at the mouth!

This is it, I thought. *Thanks, Dad.*

I lined him up in my sights, balanced on the balls of my feet, and kicked upwards with the pointed toe of my silver stiletto.

Whammo! Target! Breachey dropped to the floor.

Not so hard, I thought as I turned nonchalantly back to the bar.

The bowlo manager called the ambulance. Breachey was taken to Cooma hospital.

Two days later, he was back at the Jindy pub.

"Sorry, Mum," he said.

Heavens! I thought. *I have come up in the world.*

Breachey and I had entered another phase of our relationship (if it could be called that). He became an employee of the hotel and was absolutely brilliant as a brown snake catcher, and there were plenty of those around the pub!

The Night of the Long
White Fence Palings

Bombala is a small town in the Southern Ranges not far from Bega, and halfway from the coast to Canberra. It is a pretty town surrounded by peaceful, green rolling hills, with a river meandering through it. Bombala was a timber town and my father, Jack, who was the personnel officer for the Forestry Commission, used to go there regularly when the timber industry was in full swing. He always said how picturesque it was and he did not exaggerate. Sadly, Bombala got much smaller in population when the timber industry dwindled.

The night I arrived Bombala was still small, but it was not to remain peaceful that Friday night, nor the following Saturday night. I was there with a group of racehorse owners. The syndicated horse was Floppy Disk, trained by local legend, Barbara Joseph. We were a new syndicate of about five owners and were there to have a look over the stables, have lunch with Barbara and generally get to know one another. We had never met each other before, had no idea of anyone's background or what type of person each of us was. As it turned out, there were two publicans in the group: Brian and Morris. I wasn't regarded as a publican—the male half was there and he was it. Women were just the other half of the team in those days.

Saturday night we found ourselves at the Imperial Hotel where we all had booked rooms. The night started calmly enough. After we had each checked in, we met at the bar, as you do, where we chatted and got to know each other while waiting for Barbara and her husband, Peter. Brian and Morris were both delighted that they were in the same trade, and soon the stories flowed faster than the beer!

Eventually we sat down at the dining room table: we were the only diners there, which was a good thing as inevitably the conversation got a lot louder. Dinner was good, typical country-pub fare—tomato soup, roast lamb with homemade gravy, baked veges, cauliflower and white sauce, followed by bread and butter pudding and peaches. It was all washed down by copious amounts of beer, and red and white wine. The obvious thing to do after the meal was to adjourn to the public bar. So we did. Brian the Publican and Morris were in full voice!

About 10 p.m., the hotel owners retired to bed. *A bit strange,* I thought. *It's Friday night, one of the busiest nights for a pub.* It was even stranger because the barmaid was a young girl of about 22. On a busy night like this, she needed some help, preferably male. These were the first two sins committed by the licensee, but the third sin was unforgiveable. It was an unwritten rule, back then, that if there was another publican on the premises, you sat with them for a while, had a few beers with them and made sure you paid for the majority of beers. Didn't happen, but the group was getting on so well that this wasn't really noticed.

At 11 o'clock, curiosity got the better of me. I asked the young barmaid why the owners were not there.

"We always have trouble on a Friday night," she said.

"What!" I exclaimed. "And you're here all by yourself?"

"That's okay," she replied. "If things get too bad, I duck down behind the bar."

By this time things were getting a bit busier, so I offered to get the drinks for our group and ring up the money on the till. She was happy with this. So I had done this a couple of times when 11.30 p.m. arrived. The doors to the public bar flew open and in walked six big Maoris. They got their drinks and headed for the pool table. Within two minutes of their arrival, the music behind the bar had increased to a thumping crescendo.

This is not on, I thought. I hate loud music. So I went up to the bar to tell the barmaid to turn it down. She was nowhere in sight. She hadn't ducked behind the bar. She had disappeared. Forgetting that it was not my pub, I pulled up the bar flap, walked in and found the volume control. I turned it down.

"What do you think you're doing?" yelled one huge, tattooed Maori. "Turn it up. We like it loud."

"That's what you think," I muttered as I calmly walked over to the pool table. "Look here, guys," I said to the huge one, "that volume is staying where it is. It would be better if you bought me a red wine and we all had a game of pool. You finish the game you're playing. Pick a partner, I'll pick a partner and we'll play you for drinks. I'll just wait here until my red wine arrives."

He looked at me (I think he saw or heard his mum in me), and

212

then I looked around for a partner. He put down his cue and headed over to the bar to get a wine for me. The barmaid had deemed it safe to return. Wine in hand, I went over to our corner to find one of the guys ready to risk his life. The one who came, Joe, was probably the one who had the most Dutch courage. We played the game. We lost. I like to think it was a diplomatic loss. After a few more drinks, Joe and I rejoined our group.

Morris, the other publican, said to me, "You run a good pub. I didn't think you had much chance when you approached those Maoris."

"It's not my pub," I said. "I just can't stand loud noise and the young girl behind the bar was petrified. Someone had to do something." I was thinking, *None of you guys had the gumption!*

In retrospect, they were a lot wiser than me. The Maoris were there for a purpose. They were looking for a rival group and were going to give them a hiding. Luckily, their rivals were not there that night! The Maoris came back on Saturday night with the white pickets they had ripped off someone's fence and the hotel became a bloody battlefield. Police had to be called to break it up. I think the battlefield would have occurred earlier on Friday night if one of the men had approached them as I had.

Female publicans can tread where brave men fear to go.

Who's Been Sleeping in My Bed?

Things were fabulous at the LJH before I got there. Fabulous, that is, for everyone but the owners. A drinker's heaven on earth. There was a scheme implemented once upon a time that kept the patrons very happy. I exposed this utopia, and I was not popular. To keep a business viable, wages have to be kept to maximum 18 per cent, and this included management staff. Especially so in a seasonal hotel, where winters were very, very good financially and summers were very, very bad. So of necessity I had been looking at operations and ways to make them more efficient.

I looked at the housekeeping wages. They seemed too high when I applied the formula that I had been taught at Ryde. This was that an "out", a room that the guest was leaving, would take 20 minutes to clean, and a "stay", a room in which the guest would be occupying another night, would take 10 minutes to clean. The time required was, in part, dependent upon the preparations that the housemaid had made to her cleaning trolley prior to beginning to clean her allotted rooms. There was a formula for this also. This formula took into account time to load the trolley and the number of product items put on it. So, for example, for ten rooms—four outs and six stays—it would take two and a half hours, including about 10 minutes to load the trolley. The formula for the trolley was X number of sheets, pillowcases, towels, and "giveaways". (Giveaways are the soaps, shampoos and shower caps that are found in the bathroom. There were so many giveaways per completed trolley. There were also biscuits, tea and coffee.) The strict count of items on the trolley was meant to eliminate theft. This count was checked by the housekeeper. Cleaning product was also measured, recorded and doled out by the housekeeper. And the housekeeper at Jindabyne was good. My children still make their beds with "Cheryl" corners, tight and without a wrinkle, top sheet turned over twice at the top.

The number of rooms to be cleaned was the number of outs or stays recorded in the reservation book at the front office. Computers were just starting to be used then. The housekeeper would collect the handwritten list and allocate rooms so that each housemaid got roughly the same number of hours. But try as we might, there always seemed to be 20 minutes or so of unaccounted time, usually at the weekends. The only way to solve this was to supervise the girls as they worked, as well as for the housekeeper to check each room that was completed. Everything seemed to be going well and everyone seemed to be industrious and all were working to schedule.

But something was going on—the block opposite the public bar always seemed to take longer than it should. I asked the housemaids if they knew anything. The beds had been slept in, but the bathrooms hadn't been used, nor anything used in the bathroom except the toilet. No, nobody knew anything. I decided to say nothing for the next few days. I'd learned by this time that there was a lot more going on in more ways than I knew.

It was a puzzle until my old schoolfriend Sue alerted me. Sue and her husband, Manfred, had been painting the rooms and Sue went to the end room of the block to open up and cover furniture. Manfred was wandering along with paint and ladder, when he heard the loud scream. He was 188cm, solid, not afraid of a scrap, so he continued along, a bit faster, to investigate. Sue had found that the unoccupied room, was occupied. She had hotfooted it to the office by the time Manfred got to the room.

"Lyn, I've solved the mystery of those rooms. Some of the drinkers are using them to sleep off their hangovers and leaving through the back window." Sue still vividly recalls seeing a bare bottom squeezing out the window, trousers and shoes in hand, heading bare-arsed for the lake.

The story went around town. You would think this was the end of it. Not so. Some men are slow learners. There was one last attempt to use the "sleep it off" area. The next weekend I decided to check on Friday morning. Nothing. Rooms as they should be. Saturday morning still okay. Sunday… not okay. As I approached the last two rooms, I saw the curtains were drawn and there were keys in both doors. I knew those rooms had not been booked. We had a policy of booking them last in summer as the public bar was the noisiest part of the hotel at that time of year and our guests were booked into the quieter end adjacent to the office.

Right, I thought. *This time I'll really get to the bottom of this.* I threw open the door and found one of my better public bar customers sleeping it off, or he had been.

"What in the hell do you think you're doing? Get up, get out and don't come back."

I could have been heard in Cooma. I was heard next door. The door to that room crashed open and another good customer was scrambling up to the bar. So I followed him up. He had the good sense to run right through the public bar and across the main road. Good thing nothing was moving on the highway.

I was livid. I didn't have to say anything to anyone. Word got around: "She knows."

I thought that would be the end of it. It was the end of the free sleep-offs and almost the end of me. I wasn't the most popular person in Jindabyne, and it was time for a fearsome foursome of the patrons to let me know I had no right to change things. A deputation confronted me in the dark, deserted entertainment room one stormy night. With the rain on the roof and the noise from the late Friday night drinking crowd, I heard nothing as I did the saloon bar stocktake. But I soon felt something.

"We want to see you," said one of the avenging four cowboys as they spun me around. I should have smelled their beery breaths. "We are going to teach you a lesson that you won't forget. Think you can come in here and change what we have been doing for years?"

Well yes, actually, I did.

"We're going to teach you a lesson you won't forget," another repeated. "Three of us will hold you down and the other one will bruise a few ribs." Whether it was bravado or the grog talking, I didn't wait to find out. Attack is the best form of defence, so attack I did.

"Listen, you guys," I grated out, index finger pointing. "Lay one finger on me and I'll make sure you end up in Goulburn jail, you bastards. I have a few mates in there. Some of them are never to be released, so they will be waiting for you. They will be happy to do me a few favours. Each one of you will have his skin taken off inch by inch with a rusty razor blade, and then they will make lampshades out of it."

They looked at each other and then at me. I hadn't been nicknamed "the little bantam" years ago for nothing. I was ropeable and way beyond any fear. They decided that retreat was a good option

As I watched their slinking backs I thought, Thank God they hadn't read Hitler's *Mein Kampf,* or I wouldn't have gotten away with that bluff.

The Ghost at The Lake Jindabyne Hotel

The hotel workers were comfortably sitting at the end of the long public bar. The lights were off. It was winter. It was "staffy" time. The conversation was low, the level of exhaustion high. The public bar had been packed that night, the demand for drinks relentless. Norts, the chef, was about to push his glasses up the bridge of his nose, stare through them and utter a pearl of wisdom when— Crash!—followed by an even louder scream. We heard racing footsteps and panting noises, and then a figure blasted through the swing doors into the safety of our group. It was the useful, who was a bit slow wiping down the tables in the band room after all the patrons had left, and had been finishing off by himself. The premises had been checked. No patrons remained.

"There's somebody in there," he gasped, eyes like saucers. He grabbed the nearest beer, which happened to be Norts' schooner.

"Not so fast, mate." Norts grabbed the schooner back in alarm. "That's just old Fred."

Most hotels have a ghost, an entirely logical state of affairs when you realise that the hotel is a life within its own walls. Some ghosts are barely alive. They're the regulars: white, drawn, and scarcely there until the day after a heavy night, when they return for their "heart-starter" (usually a beer, a shandy or a rum) and come alive again. Then there are the "real" dead—the ones who didn't want to leave. Why would they? They had happy memories of the place, and continued to have them. This could not be said for those who were on the hysterical end of their pranks. These people had a healthy fear of what they couldn't see or understand. I didn't have a problem with long-gone patrons who'd become ghosts—after all, I'd met a few—but not everybody could say "Gidday" to the space they were probably occupying, smile, perhaps make a comment, and then go about the day's or night's work.

Fred, as he was affectionately known to the locals when he was alive, had been closely associated with the pub, having worked there for many years before he died. He was everything to the place: PR man, drinker, cleaner, father confessor, the shoulder to lean on, and to his credit he took all his confidences to the grave. Maybe he thought he was owed a bit for all the good work he had done above and beyond the call of duty, and set out to have a good laugh. So he had his fun at night, either when staff were cleaning up, or when all had gone home and the place was empty. The LJH was a huge hotel for him to roam around mischievously. And roam he did, particularly the bars and restaurants. Two of his favourite tricks are embedded in my memory. I loved him for them.

At night, the staff always clean tables, ashtrays and the bar. If left dirty, the hotel soon smells and becomes a home for bar flies— not the patrons, the real ones: the small black flies that live on sugar. The tables and bar area have to be wiped down with warm soapy water. (I think soapy water does a better job than chemicals, and it is much cheaper.) The ashtrays have to be emptied and wiped clean with a wet cloth, taken to the bar, and put through the dishwasher as the last items cleaned.

As the LJH was an old hotel, there was a trough around the bar. This had to be swept. Last job was the bar towels, which had to be taken downstairs to the dim, dungeon-like area beside the wine cellar, and the first load started in the washing machine. So Fred had plenty of scope and time for his tricks.

This night, Fred had pulled his favourite upstairs winter trick. This one got the staff a few times before comprehension dawned. One staff member would go into the entertainment area to wipe down the tables and ashtrays before taking them to the public bar, where staff members were cleaning up. Fred would strike. An ashtray would fall off the table and hit the floor with a solid bang. These were large, thick glass ashtrays, about 16cm^2. They were big, ugly and heavy because this was the Snowy Mountains, party capital of Australia during the winter, and being so big and ugly, they were less likely to walk out in someone's bag to grace a rental unit. They didn't shatter, but made a hell of a noise. Imagine you are a staff member and an ashtray falls off the table behind you. You look around, think nothing of it and continue working. Then it happens again. You'd wonder what you were doing wrong. It happens a third time. You begin to more than wonder, so you hurry, finish up, and return to the safety of fellow staff and bright lights in the public bar. You take someone back with you to turn off the lights. Not really scared yet.

Now Fred wasn't stupid. Nothing else would happen that night, or for a few after. Then, the same thing happened again.

The bar staff member cleaning up would have a logical thought. A door has been left open at the side of the area. Shouldn't be. Not safe for staff in case of robbery, and an open invitation for a patron who knows the ropes to duck in and grab a few bottles. He checks. No door open. Odd. Then there is a loud crash behind him. Another ashtray hits the floor. Again, the guy hits the public bar running.

"I'm not going in there by myself. Someone's there. One of you will have to come in and help me clean up."

In comes the mate. Nothing. Uneventful. But then it happens again the next night. The staff are spooked. No one goes out to the back bar alone. Two bar staff clean, all lights on. The kitchenhand in the bistro wants a useful with him as he cleans. All lights on. And so the legend of the LJH ghost continues.

But so far so good downstairs. Thoughts of Fred remain upstairs. Then strange things begin to happen down below. His modus operandi has changed. Nothing daunts Fred.

Each night after closing, the Thai restaurant is turned into the breakfast room and the tables have to be reset for breakfast. Usually two staff do this at close of restaurant trading, but one day, a month into winter, the breakfast staff came to see me with a complaint.

"Lyn, you'll have to speak to the night staff. The breakfast tables aren't being set properly. The knives, forks and spoons are in the wrong order, and sometimes they are so lazy they just leave everything heaped in the middle of the table."

Didn't sound like the restaurant staff, but I had a word anyway.

"Lyn, when we leave, everything is set correctly. Check if you like, but you'll find it all good."

I checked. It was good. Everything was in order. Things were peaceful for a while, but Fred got bored, or maybe he was aiming for maximum effect. One night a table setting of four crashed to the ground behind the staff resetting. Panic. Fred had struck. They knew what had happened upstairs. So repeat of upstairs—all lights on, always two staff in restaurant, and the kitchenhand in the kitchen made sure he left when they left.

Fred sure brought action to the pub. Maybe he had the welfare of the pub and the wages bill in mind? It certainly meant no staff dallied longer than they had to. Clean up, drink up and leave. I have it on good authority that Fred is still heard on cold winter nights and is even sometimes seen. Was it him that a guest saw disappearing through a door in the pool area late at night, or imagination fuelled by too much spirit out of a bottle?

The Responsible Service
of Alcohol Course

Throughout my 40 years in the pub game, I've spent a lot of time training, teaching and lecturing in hospitality.

At one stage I conducted a 16-week hospitality school at the Lake Jindabyne Hotel for Tourism Training Australia. It was the first training school in the Snowy Mountains, and it was at this course that RSA (Responsible Service of Alcohol) training was trialled. It was here that the RSA slogan "No more. It's the law" was first coined; it first appeared in *The Summit Sun* on 4 July 1996, (on the following page) and has since been adopted throughout Australia.

The first area-wide training session of RSA involved all licensees of pubs, clubs, restaurants and bars in Jindabyne, Thredbo, Perisher and Blue Cow. It was a pretty intensive course spread over two days. The usual course took only six hours. This one was longer because of the increased police presence over the ski season—the police force was bolstered at this time with extra uniformed police on the roads and at stations, and extra undercover police on premises and in cars with video cameras. The licensees were concerned. If there were underage patrons on the premises and they were inadvertently served, the licensee would be in court. Similarly, if an intoxicated patron was videoed leaving the premises, the licensee would be in court. There were no on-the-spot fines at this stage.

NO MORE
IT'S THE LAW

RESPONSIBLE SERVICE OF ALCOHOL
- Our responsibility to the -

RESPONSIBLE DRINKERS	THE COMMUNITY THE LAW	IMMEDIATE NEIGHBOURHOOD

1. PREVENT - under age drinking

2. PREVENT - or manage intoxication and intoxicated behaviour

3. PREVENT - drink driving

4. PREVENT - or manage violent behaviour

5. REFUSE - entry or service to any persons displaying signs of intoxication

The responsible service of alcohol policy is followed by these establishments:

 LAKE JINDABYNE HOTEL

 BALCONY BAR & RESTAURANT

 BRUMBY BAR & BISTRO

 HORIZONS RESORT

 ASPEN HOTEL MOTEL

 MARIO'S MINESHAFT RESTAURANT & BAR

 AZIFAZ

JINDABYNE BOWLING & SPORTS CLUB

Proudly supported by the Summit Sun

SUMMIT SUN, Thursday, July 4, 1996 — 7

Consequently, the course attracted all the licensees—not all of whom were fond of each other. With the mixture of nationalities and personalities who were represented, the situation had the potential to explode.

The course started at 10 a.m. Half an hour beforehand a friendly, happy bunch were sipping coffee and tea, hoeing into the biscuits and sandwiches, and exchanging gossip. The course was held in a downstairs meeting room that had been set up with a video television, a whiteboard, an easel with butcher's paper, and a projector. There was no Microsoft PowerPoint back then, so a fair bit of equipment was needed.

"Hey, Lyn," called Sid the Hungarian. "All right if we have a beer?"

"No," I replied. "This is about the responsible service of alcohol, and it may as well start now. No alcohol now, at lunch, or during the course." I said "alcohol", as "beer" would automatically be translated into the tipple of choice: whisky, rum or wine. With the ground rules set, it was time to start.

It was an interesting course. There were serious parts—the Health Act, the Liquor Act—which had to be taught in a fairly dry way, and then there were the humorous aspects that were made clear by using cartoons as illustration. How the human body absorbs alcohol was always well-received. The size of the body is a determiner, but the most important thing is the liver—some people can absorb their drinks effectively over a time interval, others cannot.

Thus the course, with its factual information bolstered by stories, progressed happily along until lunchtime.

We had lunch on the LJH premises. I had lunch with them. No one wanted to miss Nort's legendary cooking! His steaks were to die for, and he had a far-flung reputation for his homemade pies! No one had a drink. Down we went for the second session.

The second session was the most important for all of us. We were determined that we would not contravene the law by serving intoxicated persons. No one wanted to appear in court. It was expensive in terms of legal cost and time. The court was in Cooma, so it meant getting a solicitor, trips to Cooma, and then the actual court costs.

So we came up with a plan. Security outside was not the big issue that it is now. Some premises didn't need it; some did. There were two strategies to our plan inside the premises. The first strategy involved the useful who picked up glasses. He constantly walked around and could monitor the patrons. If he saw anyone he thought should not be served another drink, he would notify the bar staff and point out the group: person, friends and location. (Mind you, the LJH public bar was so big and held so many people that we employed one staff member, Carmel, whose only job was to liaise with staff and the useful!)

The useful also had to record all incidents that happened on the premises in an incident book that was kept behind the bar— with the name of the patron who was to be refused service, a description of the person, and the time refused. Then it was time to ensure that friends didn't buy a drink for their mate. This was time-consuming, but paid dividends. No group of friends wanted to be asked to leave—especially when it was snowing outside. Staff were also instructed to look for undercover police. It was better to be prepared than to be copped!

The second strategy was bar sections. The outside bar area was divided into sections. Each member of staff behind the bar was given a section to keep an eye on during the night. If they spotted patrons they thought had had enough to drink or might cause trouble by their behaviour, they alerted the manager, who would go and handle it. This way, trouble did not start. Also, if a patron was asked to leave, the manager had to escort them to the door and note the direction they walked in. This also had to be written in the incident book. The manager also had to monitor the doorway at intervals. With the police often outside in their cars with video cameras, it was imperative that a patron did not leave with a glass in his or her hand. This was an offence. In time, at the LJH we employed a staff member just to monitor this at the doorway.

But the most important aspect was licensee looking after licensee. We instigated a system that day, which worked very well for us—too well, I'm sure, as far as the police were concerned. We made up a list of the premises in Jindabyne. As soon as a patron had been refused service in one premise, and had left the premises, a call was made to the next premise on the list to pass on the time of leaving, a description, and the direction this patron was headed. That licensee then phoned the next licensee and alerted them, and so it went on down the list. This worked extremely well in Jindabyne. The LJH, the Jindabyne Bowling Club, the Balcony Bar, the Snowy River Hotel, Mario's Italian Restaurant, AZIFAZ, the Brumby Bar were all within walking distance, so the patron had no hope. If I recall, hopefully correctly, there were no arrests on the premises for intoxication—except for me! I was charged with a member of my staff serving an underage, intoxicated patron at approximately midnight one Friday night. The patron was on the dance floor. He "was weaving around, dancing erratically and bumping into people". My staff disputed this. The case went to Cooma Court where it was found in the photographs taken as evidence of the offence committed were not of my premises. How could this happen? Maybe our system was too good and an incident was needed to help police morale?

I went on to conduct RSA courses throughout NSW, including the first course for club managers only, at the invitation of John Henry, who was the manager at North Sydney Leagues Club.

All the courses were interesting, but two stick in my mind. One was at Cooma for licensees. I walked into the room at the hotel to find that most of the licensees were sitting having a schooner and a cigarette. I very kindly delayed the start until they had finished both, and informed them that the course was alcohol- and smoke-free. Coughing and spluttering, they thought I was a bit harsh!

The second was in Jindabyne. As continuing "protection' for ourselves, the licensees had a meeting to get up to speed on what was happening around town and how our RSA initiatives were going. They all had a beer and cigarette during this one. Coffee wasn't so popular! Anyway, during the course of this a restaurant owner, Giovanni, the "Italian stallion", accused Amira, the "fireball Lebanese nightclub owner", of stealing his patrons while they, the patrons, were waiting for a table in the foyer of his restaurant.

"You come into my restaurant. You take my customers into your nightclub and sell them Lebanese food. I will have no money. You take the food out of the mouths of my wife and children!"

"You slashed my tyres Friday night. I couldn't drive home," said Amira. "My brother had to come from Cooma to take me home!"

"You threw the bricks through my windows. I know it was your brother, Amira."

With that, Amira saw red. She jumped up, ran around the table, and landed a fabulous punch on Giovanni's face. He went down for the count. All we could hear was, "You have ruined my face! Who will look at me now?"

Amira got in, "Nobody ever wanted to look at you in the first place, you ugly pig!" before she was pulled off Giovanni.

This feud had been bubbling for months and provided lots of interest in town. When Giovanni's hot water went off at crucial trading time, it was Amira. When Amira's lights went out at midnight, it was Giovanni. Retribution followed retribution. Threat followed threat.

There was nothing for it—time for a few drinks and calming of the waters. The few drinks went on for a few hours. Nobody left. They thought there might be another aria in this grand opera. How disappointing it was when Amira bought a bottle of the best red and shared it with Giovanni as a peace offering!

We could now all worry about our RSA without any further entertaining diversions at meetings—a sober but true fact for the rest of the ski season.

The Guest Who Stepped In
From the Cold

Although I wasn't liked too well in Jindabyne, there was one incident when I thought I would get my own back. Fair is fair, but underhand is over the odds. The crowd at this party will be anonymous. The setting was the end of winter. The place was the Verandah Bar, which was just across the highway from the pub.

It appears I had been doing too good a job with the trialling of "Responsible Service of Alcohol", as some sections of the public, patrons included, and my hotel had been wrongly targeted and photographed by a disgruntled punter as an establishment that allowed one underage drinker onto the premises. Although, as mentioned, this had been proved untrue in court, it took time, effort and money to substantiate this.

I decided to retaliate. As a publican's wife, I was a known character in Jindabyne, but far from a colourful one as the term is applied and generally understood by most Australians. There were plenty of these characters who could have been targeted—those who lived in the hills and only came to town to get supplies of food and alcohol and then disappeared again for an unspecified amount of time until their supplies ran out; artists escaping their confining past lives; those who were known for scams; those who were evading debts and had changed their names (nobody had any idea who these were; they had been there so long under their assumed names: the whisper around town was generally that they owed debts on the racetrack or money to the taxman). Then there was the shady Sydney character who made a living in summer by shooting porno movies in his establishment. But no, it was me who was the target.

I got the whisper that a few of these characters and punters who had targeted me were having a "Farewell to the Snow Season" at the bar over the road one Sunday night, and a very quiet whisper about what was going to be the entertainment. Late on Sunday afternoon, I checked. Sure enough, the windows of the bar were blacked out with garbage bags and there was a big sign: "Private Function".

Got them, I thought.

Discretion being the better part of valour, I asked our chef, Norts, to accompany me. Norts was a real local, and I was somewhat local now, so two well-known persons had a fair chance of getting into the function. I didn't tell Norts my plan. I certainly didn't tell him I planned on taking a camera or that I was bent on revenge. I just asked him if he would come across with me at around 11 p.m.

He did.

All went according to plan. The outside of the Verandah Bar was dark. We knocked. The glass door quietly opened a crack. No light was emitted. The doorman's head peeped cautiously out. Another local.

"Hi Lyn. Hi Norts. Come in. Don't know if it's really the place for you, Lyn, but have a few drinks anyway."

We went to the bar, peering into the cigarette-smoke-filled gloom. Just as our eyes were growing accustomed to the darkness, the smoke, and the pack of men, a cheer went up. I could just make out a skinny bloke wearing only underpants, seating himself in a chair. The very bloke I wanted to get. Suddenly, a naked woman appeared out of the fog and sat on his knee. Better than I had anticipated. Never in my wildest dreams did I really think that this was what I would walk into: a no-holds-barred men's night. I surreptitiously got out the camera (didn't have to be too surreptitious: the minute the naked woman walked through the room, all eyes were on the tableau about to unfold). Giving them a few moments to get into a compromising position, the girl straddling his knees, him grinning like a Cheshire cat, I moved into camera position, and snapped. It didn't have much effect on the room—strobe lights were dancing crazily around, so one more flash meant nothing. But the man in the chair saw me.

"Quick, Norts, we're off."

Norts stared at me through his glasses, pushed them further up on his nose. By this time they were getting fogged up, either with the atmosphere or the sight before him.

"Hurry up, Norts. We're out of here."

With that, I grabbed him and dragged him as fast as I could to the door, at the same time managing to get his half-finished schooner out of his paw. We hotfooted it across the road and just

233

made it to the other side as I heard the glass door to the Verandah Bar crash open and the skinny bloke lurched out.

"Thanks, Norts, I'm okay now. I'm home."

The door to the manager's flat was only 20 yards away. I fumbled the key into the lock and slammed the door. Thankfully there was no pounding on the door, only a plaintive voice in the icy night air.

"You can't do that. Give me that film."

No way, mate, I thought. *I've got it and I'll keep it.*

I slept the sleep of the just.

The next morning at 7 a.m. there was a banging on the flat door.

"Lyn, open up."

I did.

"You can't keep that film. I need it. I'll lose my job if it gets out."

"You didn't think about my livelihood when you set out to frame me. Bad luck. I haven't got the film. It went into Cooma this morning. One copy is going to a lawyer there, one has been posted to my lawyer in Sydney, and one to my bank manager." I was still furious and didn't care about the pathetic figure looming in front of me. With that, I slammed the door.

I heard from him a few years ago and he asked me again for the film.

"Fair go, Lyn. I've been on stress leave. It can't matter now. It was years ago."

I gave him the same reply.

Pity he didn't know that I had forgotten to put in the film.

234

Aunty Lyn's Boys

There may have been a few in Jindabyne who tried to avoid me when they saw me coming, but they didn't go as far as calling me "Potholes". That was a term of endearment applied to some who locals did avoid. But we did have "Galoshes", probably named because of his smelly feet. There was the "Black Hammer". When he struck, usually at night, the encounter could be lethal. He was always on the take for a quid (dollar) or a beer. His beer fumes preceded him thankfully, and he could usually be detected and avoided. We had the "The Italian Stallion." He was the only one who thought that he merited that name, or maybe had one person in agreement, his wife. We had "Shorty", no explanation needed. Then there was "the Clocker". The rumour was that he had been a strapper who gave out a few too many tips, ran afoul of a few underworld figures, and had fled to the wilderness of the Snowy Mountains to hide. The truth will never be known, nor will his real name.

There were the many artists who lived around Kosciusko National Park. They were painters, but the story of one is probably similar to the story of many. It was said that he had a wife and five children in the Dandenongs. We knew this was true when the wife blew into town, hellbent on taking him home; however, he'd got wind of this and was long gone. All of these characters were harmless enough, and I suppose this next one was too. He was a different class of hider.

He wasn't really hiding: a few of his colourful Sydney acquaintances knew what he did in summer. In winter he was above board—he ran an accommodation venue—but he was reckoned sleazy. In summer he made porno movies, using his rooms as a locale for shoots. He was definitely one character all females in town avoided being alone in a room with. I remember one day he asked me to come and sort out a problem he had with his computer.

"You're not going by yourself," my housekeeper, Cheryl, said. She who was a force to be reckoned with. "I am going with you. Once inside a room with him, you'll never get out." She added darkly, "I know all about him."

So over we went. His eyes widened when he saw the two of us, but he didn't miss a beat as he smoothly said, "Thanks for coming, but I've fixed the problem."

"Don't think so," muttered Cheryl under her breath. "I think it was miraculously fixed when you saw me."

Others saw *me* and weren't too happy. We were the main sponsors of the local league team, the Snowy Mountains Bears. The Bears had had a losing streak and Brian thought he could end it. And he did. This happy ending entailed sponsorship money, fundraising nights, and paying and employing a coach, Mark Jones, an extremely good footballer and one of the best-looking blokes to ever don a footy jersey. If this was not enough, Brian agreed to employ a few of the footballers as doormen on our busy nights. Not being an extremely trusting person, particularly of some footballers, I laid down a few ground rules.

"Now guys, these are the rules. No alcohol before you start work or when you are working. The only soft drink you are allowed is a clear one so this means water, lemonade, soda or lemon squash. Got that?"

Nods all round. Agreement on the faces; rebellion in the hearts. Plans mentally afoot to thwart me. After 15 years in the business, by this time I knew a few tricks myself. So two weeks into the ski season, I struck. They had had enough time to feel secure in their jobs and to think that I wouldn't check up. "Check up" was my middle name. So I armed myself with a few straws. The first doorman had no drink near him, the second had a lemon squash. I bypassed this. I had my eyes on the third drink. With number two doorman watching, I approached the third drink. A coke. Obviously not meant to be there.

"Hi Gavin," I said, "what are you doing with a coke? I thought you understood that you are to have a clear drink only."

"It's all right, Lyn, I only like coke."

"Okay," I replied, "so you won't mind if I check it?" I took out a straw, put it into the drink and had a sip. Bourbon.

"You finish up now. You knew the rules. Sign off and leave the premises."

"You can't do that. I'm a footballer. The coach will be around to see you."

"Good. Now get going."

Early the next morning, the coach did come around. Trailing him were two officials.

"End of story. He's gone. No: no second chances."

Brian thought I was a bit harsh. Bad luck. Drunk doormen cannot vet patrons. Drunk doormen can't tell an inebriated patron from a sober one. Things back on track: doormen on clear drinks. All well.

Jindabyne had all types. We did know who the few good ones really were. We were lucky to have salt-of-the-earth types working for us. We had the gun fisherwoman of the Snowy region, good-looking Evie, who could out-fish the blokes and smoked a mean trout. This didn't win her too many accolades from the males. She won accolades from me, though. She didn't stand any rot in the bars. She was a good, fast worker, and even faster ticking off any customers who needed it or who had to be told to leave or wait for a while for another drink. No arguments there.

We had Norts, the legendary chef. He knew his cuts of meat as he had previously been a butcher and cooked the best steaks, exactly as ordered. Some nights in winter he had 40 on the grill at once. He never made a mistake. I had a bit of trouble persuading him to cook a meat pie, though. I had to cook the first lot and take the finished product to bar customers to sample. These pies were huge, high and full of chucks of beef in a red wine jus. At the end of the first winter, patrons were ordering dozens to take back with them to Sydney. Norts' enthusiasm for this culinary delight waxed and waned. When it waxed, he was gung-ho making beef and burgundy pies, steak and kidney, mixed beef, and his own special, chicken and leek. When it waned, I was making them.

Norts was notorious for having a few drinks and having a lay down on the nearest available lounge before starting a shift. His loyal staff loved him and always rallied round as part of the super bistro team. A much-liked character. My most vivid memory of Norts is of him sitting at the end of the public bar at the end of his shift, glasses slipping down his nose, constantly pushed up with his first finger. He sat on the same stool in the same spot, winter and summer. A local attraction in summer, unofficial supervisor of bar conditions in winter. He would always do glass rounds whenever he thought they were needed. Everyone would talk to Norts in all situations except one—when he was eating a blue steak (a steak that has been cooked by searing on the outside only to seal in the juices). He could always talk the leg off an iron pot, which was okay, but not when the blood from the blue steak was dripping down his chin. Then he was avoided like the plague. I can't praise Norts enough. He always had the welfare of the pub foremost in his mind, even when I had to have a hard talk with him about his rest periods.

Another loyal character was Breachey. We had our differences. The Snow Ball incident was one, but after the Snow Ball incident when he thought he would kill me, and after he had finished his stint as a "Stop and Go" man for the road repairs on the Alpine Way (the road to Victoria past Thredbo), he thought he would like to work at the pub. It defies comprehension as to why I employed him, but I was glad that I did. Breachey always wore his cowboy hat and boots, and was a willing hand at any work—gardening, sweeping, bringing in kegs—but the two duties he excelled at were greeting and farewelling tour buses, and killing brown snakes.

The tour buses would pull up. Breachey and I were always there to greet them cheerfully, big smiles on our faces. The hotel in summer would not have survived without this clientele. In sweeps the tour bus, 40 eager or tired, happy or unhappy, faces peering out from their high perches: peering down at me and Breachey as I gave them a welcoming spiel. I would explain that Breachey would take their luggage to their rooms, I would tell them when dinner was, and then give them their keys. There was a bit of a contrast in my appearance to that of Breachey. I would be the official-looking chatelaine: dress spotless, hair tidy, make-up on. Contrast that with Breachey: scuffed cowboy boots, work-stained jeans, check shirt, large leather belt, Stetson pushed back on head.

Then a loud voice would ask: "Where's the list for the bags, Mum?"

You could see the weary older travellers trying to comprehend the relationship. I looked like the evil stepmother of Cinders exploiting my own child. However, by the next day when Breachey, Brian and I were there to farewell the group, they had usually asked the bus driver or worked things out for themselves.

I was glad they were not there when Breachey was busily engaged in ridding the place of any brown snakes that may have been unsuspectingly sunning themselves. The Lake Jindabyne Hotel was situated on the lake. A big body of water: requisite number one. A large expanse of lawn for sunning. Two large carparks: beautiful hot asphalt. Heaven for the browns. If they weren't in the laundry, cosy beneath the washing machines or dryers, they were dozing on the grass or the concrete strip in front of the motel rooms.

The phone would ring in the office.

"There's a brown snake in front of room 8."

"Breachey," I would yell, "there's a snake in front of room 8."

He would down tools from whatever he had been doing and streak past the office on his way to the motel rooms. Breachey didn't necessarily need a stick to immobilise a snake. Somehow he walked up, bent down, grabbed it behind the head and into a hessian sack before the snake realised that his idyllic slumber was at an end. Both Breachey and snake would disappear in the ute for a bit of bush out of town. Joking aside, brown snakes were a common problem and there was rarely a day in summer when one or a few weren't sighted and caught.

I do remember with great clarity one day when some baby browns had hatched and decided to move. It was three in the afternoon on a hot summer's day. I was on reception. A guest from Sydney had arrived to check in. I sat at the desk, smile ready to be whipped out. That smile waited awhile. The guest got out of his car and had one foot on the step. That foot froze, the other didn't follow, and a look of horror appeared on his face. That was a far as the facial muscles got. No sound passed his lips. After a few minutes I thought I had better get up and see what had happened. Smile on face, I opened the door. I looked towards the guest and then saw what had immobilised him. Six little baby browns had started their journey into the big world. Even at that early stage, their heads were raised and they were poised to strike. They must have been under the front steps. I remember wondering where the mother was.

"Just stay there," I said. Probably the instruction should have been, "Slowly back away". "Breachey!" I yelled at the top of my voice. "Browns."

The snake catcher supreme miraculously appeared, sack in hand, and easily picked them up. Like watching a slow-motion silent movie, when the browns disappeared, movement again resumed. The mother never appeared. I wonder if the guest ever made a return stay.

Now it is time to introduce Scaras. A true Jindabyne legend if ever there was one—and there probably never will be another Scaras. While to Breachey I was "Mum", to Scaras I was "Aunty Lyn", and I was the supreme boss. It was believed, in one hot gossip version or another, true or untrue, that Scaras, all 170cm, 52kg wringing wet, had turned up one winter fresh from the countryside of Victoria, where he was known as a champion squash player. Scaras loved what he saw in Jindabyne and he loved a drink. He needed an income to stay in this idyllic place. He hit upon an idea. He got a job as a caretaker of a hall.

All went well until winter came and his original idea germinated into a fantastic one. He was caretaker of this hall. The hall was closed at night. He could keep it open at night as a backpacker's, one night at a time, charge rent, and bring in a tidy income. All went well for the first season, but unravelled on the second. The word went around among the backpackers and eventually reached the ears of the owners. Scaras was out.

What to do? Employment at the pub looked good. He was in.

We were the third pub owners to inherit Scaras. Every pub has a Scaras, a character who is unique and who likes a drink. When we arrived in the late '80s, Scaras was an institution and lived at the caravan park. He had an ideal set-up there. The caravan was the right size, fulfilled his needs and soon fulfilled another. Scaras loved a smoke. Why not grow his own weed? So he did.

The caravan had a skylight that could be opened to allow ventilation. This section also had a thin edging around it. Ideal for keeping dirt in. His own planter box. His own supply of weed. It is the only dwelling I have seen outside of a Neanderthal movie that has its own grass roof. He was set, everything a bachelor needed, until the night the caravan accidentally burned down.

Scaras wasn't in it. He was still at the pub.

So we inherited Scaras and I inherited a totally loyal employee. Scaras was always being sacked by Brian and being reinstated by me. This dialogue could regularly be heard.

"Aunty Lyn, Booma's (Brian's nickname, Booma, because he had a loud voice) sacked me."

"Don't be ridiculous, Scaras. He can't sack you. Go and tell him that you're not sacked." Off he went.

"You can't sack me, Booma. Aunty Lyn's the boss. She says I'm not sacked." And so it went on and on.

After his caravan burned down, Scaras had nowhere to live. By this time, alcohol had him by the throat. I came up with a brilliant plan. It had a glaring fault I didn't see.

"We have to let him sleep here at the hotel, Brian," I said. "It's winter." Fine with Brian. So I set up a living area with a bed outside the wine room and cellar—where the boiler was located, where I knew he would be warm. What a lethal combination: OH&S boiler problem, and—as Brian sensibly pointed out—access to alcohol. I pointed out that the wine room was locked, but didn't give much thought to the cellar and none at all to the boiler. After all, as far as alcohol was concerned, there were strict stock control measures in place and we'd find the bottles. At that stage I totally under-estimated the cunning of an alcoholic, and although I didn't find any evidence of drinking; I'm sure there must have been some. He knew where to hide from me when he got sick of me looking for him for something or the other, so I'm sure he had no problems with empty bottles. Also, he took the garbage out each morning. Alcoholics' heaven. I can see why he loved Aunty Lyn.

Both Breachey and Scaras remained employed by us until we sold the Lake Jindabyne Hotel. As far as I know, they were kept on by the new owners. Scaras definitely was, but his living quarters must have changed. Before we left, he agreed to come to Cooma with me for regular counselling for his alcohol problem. These sessions lasted about six months and he was just starting to look healthy and well, when he relapsed. He was drinking as heavily as ever when he visited us in Kincumber. He had hitchhiked all the way and was staying with Garry Narvo at the Bayview Hotel in Woy Woy.

Scaras has since died. A local told me that he was given a touching farewell at the hotel that he loved so much. The lounge bar, cleared appropriately, was darkened with maroon curtains. Flowers completed the look of a chapel. The dark coffin looked at home, particularly with his distinctive hat sitting atop. The service was conducted by the local Catholic priest.

"This is the first time I've conducted a service in a pub," he commented.

"Probably the last too, Father," Keith muttered

The 100 locals and his two sisters, who were there from Perth to farewell Scaras, all raised their glasses and drank a beer to the person we had all loved, who had coloured our lives so richly. He had exited the pub in style. He was always a bit of a favourite in the town and a definite favourite with me. I'll never forget the thin face atop a skinny body, greasy black cowboy hat pushed back on his head, that used to peer up at me and say, "Booma's sacked me, Aunty Lyn."

I had my own farewell drink with Scaras one winter after his death. He never did leave the pub he loved.

"Grahame," I asked the manager. "Would you get Scara's ashes out of the safe? I want to have a beer with him, outside, overlooking the lake."

I enjoyed that Toohey's New and Bundy OP chaser with one of the fast-disappearing characters Australia is so famous for.

Neigh or Nay

The Jindabyne Hotel started Brian's career as a horse owner, nay, as an owner of too many horses; and I was the one who started him on this path. It was in Jindabyne in the mid-'90s and Brian's birthday was coming up. He loved a bet, but at this stage I didn't realise how much. We had gone to the races from when we first met, and I used to have a small bet and didn't take any notice of his punting.

I got into racing in 1968. In 1966, I'd had an operation at Bankstown hospital for a torn cartilage in my right knee. In those days the whole cartilage was taken out, and there was a 9 cm scar on my right knee. The surgeon I had was ahead of his time in postoperative care: instead of leaving me in a wheelchair for a week, which was the norm then, he got me up the next day and started me walking . I was back playing tennis in six weeks. But the miracle didn't last. Just as the doctor was about to write me up in the medical journal, the knee collapsed. The verdict was no more active sport. I could swim and play a modified form of golf. I kept up the swimming, but golf wasn't my game. In 1968, I started teaching at East Hills Girls' High. One of my fellow teachers Jenny and I and would go to Canterbury after school on Wednesdays for the race meeting that was regularly held there, and often to Randwick on a Saturday. So began my interest in racing and this was an activity that both Brian and I enjoyed.

Kel Rook, an entrepreneur in Jindabyne, had an interest in racehorses. I spoke to him and mentioned that a small share in one would be a lovely surprise for Brian's birthday. He took me over to Bombala on one of my stints in Jindabyne where I met Barbara Joseph, who trained one of Kel's horses. Barbara was a lovely lady and I accordingly purchased a share in our first horse, Floppy Disk, with her. It proved to be successful and won a few races. What an unfortunate occurrence. Brian was hooked. He went on to buy shares in many more horses, all of whom, with one exception, were successful.

Brian had the luck of the Irish. Everything Barbara bought in partnership with Brian was successful, except for the one-steroid wonder. Floppy Disk started winning on Australia Day in Canberra in 1996, and then won two more sprint races in Canberra and a Class 1 race in Newcastle. In '97 and '98, we had success with a horse that had been bought from Gai Waterhouse—Flinders Street—with wins at Rosehill, Canberra, Canterbury, Warwick Farm and Kembla Grange. Impish King was another that won at Hawkesbury and Kembla Grange, and afforded us an insight into the joy of racing. One of the owners was a doctor researching nuclear medicine. After the excitement of his 50-cent each-way winning bet at Hawkesbury, he turned excitedly to his wife and said, "I'm going to get a blow-up photo of this win and hang it on our front door. Everyone will see it when they knock on the door."

"You're not," she replied in some alarm. "If it goes anywhere, it will be hung behind the toilet door."

McJoey wouldn't have been hung in the toilet. McJoey had a story to tell. He was named for McGettigan and Joseph, but as Brian had gone to St Joseph's College at Hunters Hill, the students and staff thought it had been named after the school. Whenever the horse ran, the price was short. The whole school—past and present pupils, and staff—backed it. I remember one time when they all had luck: past pupils, current teachers, brothers.

Our son, Brian, had been chosen to represent Joey's in the cricket team, so we were down in Sale for the annual Marist Cricket Carnival. Seven Marist representative teams competed from the states and territories. The boys were billeted out and the parents stayed in a motel. The last day of the match was traditionally a barbeque at one of the parent's homes. Prior to McJoey's race, Brian gave out the tip to all and sundry that McJoey could win the Sydney race. He told me when we were at the TAB, along with many parents and supporters. All had backed McJoey. I looked around at the packed TAB. What if it didn't win? Brian had no such qualm. And it won. However, Brian did breathe a sigh of relief and for the rest of the day he was the local hero. It was a memorable day. There were two wins—the horse and the cricket.

That night, a local mother at the farewell barbeque function excitedly came up to me. "Lyn, thank you. My husband gave me half of his winnings—a thousand dollars."

The husband heard this and spun around. He came hurrying up. "Lyn, I didn't tell her I had $2000 on it at 5–1."

With McJoey, we won the Frank Underwood Cup at Rosehill in 1999, and races at Hawkesbury, Wagga, Canberra and Gundagai. In 1998, McJoey won the Canberra Guineas, then it came third in the Canberra Cup behind Iron Horse. But McJoey's greatest glory was the Darwin Cup in 2001.

McJoey was a great horse. He was foaled in 1994 by White Bridle out of the mare Spectacular Lass and cost $7000, which was shared amongst the five owners. McJoey had 53 starts for ten wins and 13 placings. Not a bad record by any racehorse standards.

He was then taken to Darwin on three successive years. The first year, 1999, his jockey, Corey Brown, took ill the day of the Cup and he came second under a different jockey. In 2000, he was headed for a pothole in the sand and oil track and was pulled aside. He came second. Third time lucky.

In 2001, McJoey started at 9–2 equal favourite and won by three-quarters of a length from Heavenly Dancer, with Prince Dubai a length away third. He was ridden by David Bates, a local ride, of whom Brian said, "George Moore himself couldn't have ridden McJoey better than David Bates." High praise indeed. I remember the crowd roaring, but none more so than the owners and trainer, and Graham McNeice, who was covering the Cup.

The Darwin Cup is traditionally held the first Monday in August at the Fannie Bay Racetrack. It is a time of great celebration in Darwin. There is the Raceday ball held the weekend prior in the grounds of the Casino under the stars. There were a thousand people attending and the whole function was brilliantly organised. Long buffet tables had been set up at various points around the grounds and the alcohol was never-ending. We had fun-filled nights with the racing crowd.

Come Monday—Cup Day, a public holiday—the whole town turns out for the races. It is known as the race that "stops the Territory". The racecourse at this time was like a country track. There was no designated spot for the owners and trainers to sit. You took potluck and stood where you could. One year we were in a marquee in the middle of the track. McJoey came second. The next year we had snagged a table near the bookies, thanks to our daughter, Danielle, an old mate Denis Johns, and his mate "The Trout". McJoey came second. The year he won we were standing in front of a large video screen beside the track with Graham McNeice.

"Stand next to me, Lynnie," Graham said. Thanks to him, Brian, Danielle and I saw everything on that screen. And it was appropriate that we were with Graham. We had been friends since 1978. We all shed a tear. We were presented with the Cup and the prize money of $125,000. The Cup went to Barbara's stables in Canberra.

That night we celebrated for a short time in a Fannie Bay restaurant. For some reason the excitement was over, and Brian and I left the celebrations early. Celebrating after races is a peculiar thing. I didn't always enjoy it that much for two reasons: I was generally a bit on edge after the day, as Brian was quite a big punter and I lived in fear that he would lose a lot. The other reason was that he often copped the entire bill for the celebrating crowd, often as many as 20 people. He was a generous man, as was another owner, Morris, the hotelier from Queensland. They often paid the bill and it was never insubstantial. One incident finished me totally with some of the race crowd. It was after a successful day at Randwick and a crowd of 18 were celebrating at a restaurant in Blues Point Road, North Sydney. The best of wines and food and plenty of it was ordered by the group. Brian paid. There was no real insistence from anyone else. The glamour and excitement of racing faded for me that night.

But in all fairness, I should say that we met many wonderful people from all walks of life: fellow publicans, farmers, fishermen, politicians, businessmen, jockeys, their wives and families. It is a time of my life that I do not regret, and I am glad I experienced it. We went to racetracks all over Australia and Asia, reconnected with the racing crowd we had known for years, and went to many fabulous dinners and events such as the Gold Coast Magic Millions Carnival; the Melbourne, Perth and Adelaide Cups; the Singapore Gold Cup run at Kranji Racecourse in November; and the Hong Kong Cup.

Racing is indeed a great leveller and there is no thrill on the track quite as great as seeing your horse win.

From the High Country
To the Broadwater

Our time at Jindabyne was coming to an end. The magic ten years was rolling around and we felt the pull of a decade. Time to move. The hotel was for sale. No new destination for us as yet. A relative new chum to the game, Rick Rampling, had landed on the lawn behind the motel in his helicopter and the whole town was vibrating to the thrill of an exciting new owner. Whirling helicopter rotors would be the sound we last remembered, watching locals taken for a spin one of the last sights. At least for me.

We were still at the Lake Jindabyne Hotel when Brian got a call from a mate. As mates they went back a long way, to the days of the Henson Park Hotel when Brian was only 18 and considered a young kid behind the bar of his father's hotel, at least by the colourful characters who drank there—the underworld of the '60s that was then Sydney: George Freeman, Lenny McPherson, Abe Saffron, "Chow" Hayes, and more. He has lots of stories of this era, but they are not my stories—except for this story of his mate. They drank together at the Marrickville Tennis Club (and probably had a good idea of who robbed it in the '60s), went to parties together and to each other's weddings.

The phone call came out of the blue one morning.

"How are you, mate?" And so they chatted of inconsequential things until the reason for the call was broached. It was a tale of woe and a cry for help.

"You know a group of us bought the Kincumber Hotel, a few mates from the good old days..." Alarm bells should have rung about the mates from the good old days. "We're in a bit of trouble, mate: the bank is going to foreclose on us and sell the hotel at a fire sale unless you come in with us. The bank knows about your good record with hotels and how you can take a poorly performing one and make it profitable. The bank's terms are that you buy 30 per cent, and run it."

The figures the mate came up with looked good, but there was also fairytale stuff about boards and directors, not the stuff that pubs are made of. Pubs are basic and down to earth; money comes in, money goes out, and because it is yours, you have to make it work. There is no easy way, no magic wand that can be waved.

Knowing that there was hard work ahead of us, we arrived at the Kincumber pub in 1998.

Although he answered the call of a mate, Brian was still committed to Jindabyne for the handing over of that pub and once again, I would the one who cleaned up a new pub.

PART 7
KINCUMBER
1998–2006

Boys' Toys

Pubs, like cars and racehorses, are a magnet for "the boys". It is a dream of many men to own one and they are convinced that they are easy to run—you stand on the other side of the bar with the patrons, have a drink and the money flows in. Or so many have thought, to their detriment. Many have also thought it is the same as a club, hospital, shopping centre, or any corporate business, that it can be run through a board. Kincumber was one such pub where some of the partners thought that way.

The hotel had an interesting history. Mike Willesee had once owned the pub and the land down to the water. Situated not far from the Broadwater and beside natural bushland, it was ahead of its day in its ecological design. The hotel was a low brick building with a fair share of wood. It had a large central courtyard featuring a pergola draped with wisteria. The bars on one side and the bistro/function room on the other formed a natural windbreak, and patrons could sit in the grounds or bistro and look onto the Brisbane Waters. There was an embankment on one side of the flat lawn that had been bulldozed into shape by one of the later owners, Lindsay, who had held a rodeo there. To complete the ecological look, the hotel was surrounded by many native plants that attracted varied birdlife. It was an idyllic setting.

Back when the pub was completed, "Cheapie John" would pull up in the paddock behind the hotel every Sunday, to sell to all and sundry from the back of his truck. He was counted as part of the entertainment. Families would have barbeques and picnics there, and there would be bands. It had passed through various owners and when it ended up our hands, we wanted to bring it back to being a family place, the centre of the community. It had never been anything other than their centre in the minds of the locals. In the ten years we owned the hotel, it was never actually regarded as ours: it was theirs. The locals knew that Col Joye was a partner, so even though it wasn't "ours", they were willing to allow him a little bit of ownership. For that great honour, he had to appear there at least once a year to sing 'Bye, bye baby' and a few other golden oldies.

While the surroundings were quite beautiful, the day-to-day running of the hotel was another story. The hotel had no control systems, so the first job was to introduce these. First, we introduced a safe reconciliation sheet whereby cash, loans and petty cash were balanced. Second, we created a keg sheet to balance cellar deliveries, so that alcohol coming in, and alcohol used, could be reconciled. This measure in particular prevented theft, by preventing the giving away of alcohol. Third, we created a daily takings sheet for each department—bottle shop, bistro and bars—showing the amount taken on each shift. These were another control measure to be balanced each night before the manager left. Often they were not, and one morning I found scribbled across the sheet:

"This is fucked up. I'm leaving it."

So clampdown started.

At this point I was working 16-hour days; after six months the strain began to tell and I ended up with high blood pressure. My daughter Kate and her partner, Debbie, took a lot of the strain off me, particularly by taking over the bottle shop in the Kincumber Shopping Centre. Some staff were let go. Some were hired— notably Hazel, who was a wizard with figures and who took over reconciliation of both bottle shops. The bistro got a new menu and a new chef, Steve Jones, who was a whiz with portion control and pricing. Brian arrived. Although things had settled down and the hotel was running as a hotel should be, dark clouds were gathering on the horizon.

Gerry the Bottle-O left. Gerry had bought the hotel when he sold his bottle collection business. That business had been built up by Gerry's father about 70 years previously. Before Gerry's father started doing it, no bottles were collected from hotels. They were just thrown out. Gerry's father saw the potential in collecting them, and became very successful. So Brian knew Gerry from those '60s days: Brian helping his father, Gerry helping his.

Brian arrived from Jindabyne after he had handed over the pub to the new owner. He just got on with being the publican and let me get on with the running of the pub, the hiring and firing, and supervision of all departments.

Then we had our first meeting with the other shareholders. It was conducted as a board meeting, which is not how pubs are run. But Brian and I sat through it with amusement. We ran the pub as we saw fit. We did things our way and continued to make changes towards profitability as we always had.

Another meeting was soon called to remedy our "behaviour", where one shareholder commented, "One day you will learn how to run a pub."

We took our solicitor to the next meeting and things went from bad to worse. The less said the better.

At the first Supreme Court case, the judge ruled that the hotel had to be sold. We bought it back. The consortium refused to sell it to us. Back to the Supreme Court. The judge again ruled that the hotel had to be sold, and to us if we were the successful bidder. We were. We bought back the hotel for $6.2 million, built it up to be an extremely successful business, and sold it about seven years later for $19 million. Not bad for people who would one day "learn how to run a pub".

Many questions were unanswered about the early years at Kincumber, the main one being: "Why not let the people who know what they are doing get on with it?"

The Kids Grew Up

We got on with it and found that we had inherited lots of characters there who were personalities in their own right. Kincumber had to be turned from a bikie pub to one with a safe family environment, and quickly. All the elements to do this were already there.

I remember the first night I was there. In those days, a hotel changed hands at midday. Brian the Publican had to get back to the Lake Jindabyne Hotel, which left me running Kincumber by myself. When I was a high school teacher, I specialised in problem behaviour classes, which is where, in my opinion, the great kids are. A pub to me was an extension of the classroom; it's just that the problem kids, as well as the nice ones, are all grown up.

Things were going well until 10.30 p.m. I was in the back office balancing the bottle-shop floats. There were two bottle shops: one at the shopping centre, and a drive-through that was part of the hotel, so I had enough to do without the commotion I could hear. There were a group of about five men drinking in the saloon bar. They were the nice big kids: Roger, Bill, Rod and two others. Bill's voice was raised. He was swearing. I hate swearing. Not tolerated!

"I'm telling you mate, she doesn't look that f** tough. Let's see how she f** handles the public bar when the f** boys get in tomorrow!"

Loud laughter from the mates.

They'll find out how I handle them right now, I thought as my blood began to boil. Out I came like a Scottish terrier, straight over to their table.

"Who is that swearing? If you want to use that language, you can leave right now! There's the door—use it before I bar you!"

Barring was bad in any pub, but particularly in Kincumber. There wasn't another pub or drinking hole this side of Avoca or Erina for miles, and the barred person would have no mates to drink with. No matter how good a mate he was, he wouldn't leave "the Cucumber".

The mates laughed.

"You lot can stop that laughing! You're egging him on. One more sound and he stays and you go!"

Silence.

"And if any voices are loud enough for me to hear them in the back office, it will be a merry little band that marches out that door."

I turned and walked back to the office. I was stopped in my tracks by the look on the face of Pauline, the 153cm, 50kg bar attendant who was our ace bar cleaner. Her eyes were wide, her mouth was open, and the cleaning cloth was hanging limply in her hands.

"No one has ever spoken to them like that," she said. "No management has ever raised their voice to any patrons."

"That's why this pub has a bad reputation! Things have changed and they better get used to it. This is a family hotel from now on and those that don't like it can drink elsewhere!"

Next day, a big bunch of red roses arrived as an apology from Bill—a bunch that would arrive without fail over many years on my birthday. Those blokes turned out to be a great bunch.

I loved that pub, but there were a few more hurdles to get over.

Saturday night came. After five days I was getting a reputation. "Don't mess with the boss!" was the word that went around. At midnight I heard another commotion, this time in the public bar. I went out to see what it was about. One of the patrons, Paul, a nice enough guy with a quiet manner and a little-boy-lost smile, was staggering around with a big cut to his head and blood streaming down.

"What happened here? Who did this?" I demanded.

The three wise monkeys came into play. No one saw or heard anything or anyone. He got the cut on his head from a mysterious bolt of lightning. By the time this had been determined, he had stopped staggering and was a bleeding heap on the carpeted floor.

"Drag him out of here," I said. "He's bleeding all over the carpet. Put him outside the front door. I'll call an ambulance."

Deed done. A wet cloth was put on his head (we had some humanity), and the bleeding had stopped by the time the ambulance arrived to take him to Gosford Hospital.

Next day I said to one of the patrons who had been in the bar where Paul was drinking, "Now can you tell me what happened?"

"Yes, Lyn—he took one of the bikie's girlfriends out and the bloke found out! Bikie came in here, hit him over the head with a bar stool, and took off!"

I never did find out who the bikie was, but to this day Paul wears the scar.

The Peanut and The Head Shebang

"What in the hell are all these bikes doing here?" I said to Andy and Swanny as I looked through the door of the public bar one Sunday afternoon and saw 12 or so bikes and an equal number of leather-jacketed bikies. This was my first Sunday working after we bought the Kincumber Hotel. I was by myself. Brian the Publican was at Jindabyne, as we had just completed selling that hotel. The bikes were lined up neatly on the green grass facing the central courtyard. The boys were enjoying their bourbons and coke, and their beers.

I was still in the process of cleaning up the hotel. Its reputation was not good and we wanted to make this a safe family hotel. I later heard it was considered the third Rebels clubhouse on the Central Coast.

"This is not a pub for bikies. I'm going out to see them. There are rules—and if they don't do as they are told, they leave. We'll have a quiet chat." As I was saying this, as if by magic, all the bikies roared off on their bikes, crossing the lawn and hitting the asphalt driveway. All, that is, except one. He hopped on his bike and faced it towards the hotel courtyard.

"No, Lyn." Four hands held me back.

"Leave me alone," I said, "I'm going out there."

Out I went. By this time the tall, skinny, unshaven bikie was riding his bike around the courtyard. He had absolutely no obstructions—patrons or furniture—so he thought he would drive it through the doorway of the function room where a band was playing.

"Come here, you mug!"

He got off his bike and swaggered towards me.

I glanced back to the public bar. Forty pairs of eyes were staring at me. The band had stopped. Eighty pairs of eyes were looking from the function room, totally mesmerised.

"Who do you think you are, and what do you think you are doing?" I said as I stood on top of his size 15 leather boot and managed to look into the middle of his leather chest. Little did the big galoot realise that a 193cm brave man could have lifted his boot and sent a 153cm woman sprawling.

"I don't talk to peanuts," he said.

"I am the head shebang," I said. Poking him in the chest, I continued: "You are a peanut. Go and tell *your* head shebang that I want to talk to him."

With that, he looked at me, got on his bike and roared out of the hotel.

"Not so hard, was it?" I said, as I got back inside the public bar and was confronted by 40 pairs of eyes that were now as big as saucers. "I don't know what you blokes were worried about. They are a bunch of powder puffs." But just to be on the safe side, I spoke to the police the following day.

"They are not powder puffs," said Sarge. "You are lucky. If you had been a man, things would have been different. You would have been in hospital. It is degrading to be spoken to by a woman like that."

The following week on Sunday—family roast day—the head shebang arrived, dressed in civvies. By this time, I had spoken to the guys in the public bar and had a good idea of the relationship between the boys (I prefer that name to bikies), the pub and the community. Apparently a lot of the boys drank at the pub, as did many others who were on the periphery of the gang. As well, there were mothers, fathers, aunts, uncles, brothers and sisters of the boys who drank there. So I made sure that word got around—no "colours" to be worn (colours are the jackets you see worn with the name of the club on the back and often an insignia denoting rank), civvies only, and no bikes to be ridden to the hotel and parked there. No misbehaviour of any kind. It was a credit to the club that these rules were followed, and I went through my eight years at the hotel without trouble and with all customers indistinguishable in civvies and work clothes.

I think the head shebang came to look me over and assess the situation. He, his wife and children were pointed out to me by some of the customers. As I was working in the bistro that day, I thought the best thing to do would be to add his table to my service tables. This way I would give him the opportunity to speak to me if he wished. He didn't, even when I gave the kids their ice creams. We had a policy at that time of giving ice-cream to children dining with their families. So every opportunity was given for a chat, but this was family time and the object of the visit had been achieved.

Another day that families attended passed without a major incident. We had decided to hold a Tattoo Fair. This was a day when tattoo artists from all over the world came to show off their skills and to tattoo clients. We had artists from India, Thailand, Canada, all over Australia, as well as local Central Coast artists. It was natural that a lot of different bike groups would arrive. I had prepared for this. One section of the hotel grounds had been put aside for the bikes and I had two security guys there to make sure that their bikes were safe and secure. No colours were to be worn.

All went well and rules were observed. Kids, mums and dads, tattooed customers—all mixed easily. Hundreds of bags of hot chips were sold, hundreds of soft drinks, and naturally, hundreds of beers. The entertainment arrived. The band set up. Family groups positioned themselves on the lawn to watch the band. Wide-eyed kids had to be rounded up. Many saucer-shaped eyes were goggling, fascinated, as the artists went about their work. I continually walked around to make sure that all was running smoothly.

"Lyn," Wendy the chef's wife quietly said to me, "there are three Rebels there in the courtyard in their colours."

"Show me," I replied tersely. Rules are rules, and if it is good enough for the rest of the crowd to follow them, it's good enough for all.

There they were. Bold as brass, strutting around and drawing attention to themselves. It was not good enough. I marched up to them.

"You guys know the rules," I said. "No colours."

They looked down on me disdainfully. They were tall blokes.

"We're wearing them."

"I'll see about that," I replied and shot off to enlist help.

I was lucky enough to have the boss of the Rebels Club in Australia and his attractive wife there that day. I told him my problem.

"Where are they, Lyn?"

I took him up to where they were strutting—confidence that they could do as they liked streaming out of them.

The boss walked up. He said something. Very little actually. They left.

The Rebels have bad press. Much of it deserved. To their credit, they always behaved as gentlemen around me and in my pub.

All patrons protected their turf. To my knowledge the police conducted three drug raids with sniffer dogs on all hotels on the Central Coast during the time we had the Kincumber. I am proud to say none were found on ours. There was never any trouble at any time, and the pub continued to be a family hotel.

Tezza Two Pubs

I call him "Tezza Two Pubs" because when I first met him in one pub I thought he was just an ordinary bloke. I quickly found out that he was far from ordinary. The second time I met him he offered to kill someone who had "done me wrong". I didn't believe it, and laughed it off and forgot it, sure that he didn't mean it.

I first saw Tezza when he walked into Sheila's, a cocky bantam of a bloke, snappily dressed, hat at a jaunty angle. He was about 173cm, a thin, wiry build, with pale-blue eyes that were perpetually swivelling to survey his surroundings. "Jockey," I immediately thought. He wasn't a jockey. Brian the Publican introduced Tezza to The Boiler and me. Brian the Publican had a couple of beers with us and then left us to have a chat and a few beers with some off-duty police.

Tezza soon clarified what it was he did for a living.

"Lyn," he told me, "you knock on their door at 3 a.m. They are pretty groggy from sleep and don't think clearly. When they open the door you quickly put your foot inside so that they can't slam it. They see you standing there with a baseball bat in your hand. You slowly hit it into the palm of your other hand—whack! Whack! At the same time you look at their knees. Then you let them know what will happen if they don't have the money ready when you come back.

"You just say, 'Mate, you owe a mate of mine some money. I'll be back at five o'clock this afternoon and you'll have it ready for me.' Never had a problem getting the money, Lyn. No one wants to be knee-capped."

I bet they don't! I thought.

Well, Tezza had a few beers at Sheila's, got the taste, and then invited The Boiler and me to do a bit of a pub crawl with him and have a few drinks at the surrounding establishments. Brian the Publican declined to join us. He had work to do! The Boiler and I looked at each other and decided we were game. First we dropped in at Arizona's around the corner in Walker Street, which was run by my old mate Anthony. Then we pub-crawled down the street to Blueberries, Peanuts, and Alfred's, veered up the hill to the VC (Victoria Cross) on the corner of Pacific Highway and Mount Street, and then about-turned down Blues Point Road to the Commodore and the Blues Point Hotel, before completing the circle back at the Rag and Famish. It appeared that Tezza was well known and respected in most of these places, as I don't recall him paying for a drink. The Boiler and I managed to keep up with him in the drinks stakes, whether it was because of the fairly long walks in the fresh air or our constitutions, I don't know.

Anyway, we got back to Sheila's about midnight to find Brian the Publican and a few cops still having a drink at the bar. I suppose hard work depends on your definition of it! They all declined to approach Tezza, but as we were well into stories about Tezza's colourful past by then, The Boiler and I decided to have a few more drinks and hear a few more stories. I can understand the cops' reticence—those were the days of "live and let live". It was not uncommon then to see a policeman you knew from the local station come in with an informant. After my first faux pas of going up to the cops and their informers and asking if they would like a coffee, I was quickly told by Brian the Publican to ignore them.

"You don't see them, Lyn."

After this memorable night, Tezza passed out of my life until my Kincumber days in the late '90s. One day he suddenly appeared in the public bar. He was still snappily dressed, but some of the spring had gone out of his step. By his side was a yappy terrier, obviously the love of Tezza's life.

"Lyn, it's me—Tezza. How are you? Haven't seen you since that great night we had in North Sydney." Then, without further ceremony, "Can I have some water for my dog? He stays in the car and waits for me while I have a few drinks with my old mates."

"Hi, Tezza," I replied, stunned. "I'm well. You look as good as ever. Sure you can have some water, but bring him outside. There's a courtyard there and he can lie on the grass while we have a few drinks and catch up." Little did I know that by looking after the dog, I had won Tezza's heart!

"Thanks, Lyn. You're all right. I like anyone who looks after my dog."

So with that, Tezz and I settled down for a nice long chat about old times. After this, Tezz used to come into Kincumber every Thursday at 4 p.m., regular as clockwork. The routine never changed. Dog looked after, then Tezz, then a chat. After a few visits he met a few kindred spirits and I could leave him to tell his stories to new audiences.

After six months of this routine, he came in looking pretty serious and said, "Lyn, I need to have a quiet chat with you, somewhere where we won't be disturbed. I don't want anyone to hear me." So Tezz, dog and I headed for the far corner of the courtyard.

"Lyn, I know you bought this pub after one stint here, and some so-called mate has caused a lot of grief to you. Can't happen to a good person like you. I'm going to do something about it."

That "going to do something about it" got my antennae up. A few people had caused me a bit of grief. Part of the territory. Who did Tezz mean, or was it a someone or two or three who had also caused him some grief in the past as well? I thought that Tezz would have mellowed over ten years, but it seemed that the little bantam was raring to right past wrongs. He had one bloke in his sights.

"Now Lyn," he said. "I've sussed him out. I know where he works, when he gets there, when he leaves and the route he takes. I've followed him for weeks. All I have to work out now is how to do it."

"Tezz," I said, "I don't know what you mean by 'it'. If 'it' means hurt or kill, I don't want it. We're talking about an attempt to rob me and my family and it caused a lot of grief at the time, but justice prevailed. It doesn't mean that much to me now. It's in the past. Bad karma happens to bad people and he'll get his."

What a stupid statement. Tezz was going to ensure the bad karma happened.

Tezz had a drinking circuit. He was regular as clockwork at our hotel on Thursday, but he had other places for other days of his circuit—Woy Woy on Monday, Ettalong on Tuesday, the Union at Gosford on Wednesday, the Ocean Beach on Friday and the clubs on the weekend. The dog stayed at home on the weekends when Tezz would treat himself to a few more beers and catch the courtesy bus home. He reasoned that there were more police on the roads breathalysing on weekends. Weekdays he was safe.

After another three months of turning up on his usual Thursday, he finally told me his plan. He had worked out how to do it.

"It's all set for next Tuesday afternoon, Lyn. My mechanic mate has fixed the car. He's used to these jobs. When I put my foot on the accelerator, it shoots backwards. It will shoot towards him and he won't know what hit him. It will only take a few seconds. He passes right behind where I park the car."

"No, Tezz," I said, "I don't want you to do it. Nothing anyone does is worth killing them for."

"It is, Lyn. I've done people for less. Anyway, I've only got six months to live. I've got cancer. It doesn't matter to me whether I die in hospital or in jail." With that, Tezz and the dog left.

What will I do? I thought. *I can't let him do it. I can't tell the police yet, but I've got to tell them.* I asked Brian the Publican. He was no help. An agonising weekend followed. Monday morning arrived. At 9 a.m. I made my decision. I would ring the police at 10 a.m. and go in and see them.

Work took its usual course. Ten a.m. came and went. I forgot to call the police. The phone rang at midday. It was Veronica, the publican's wife from the Ocean Beach Hotel. She and her husband, a big bloke called Jeremy, ran the hotel, one of Tezza's regular watering holes.

"Hello, Lyn," she said. What followed was a chat about who had done what over the weekend, who was barred, and a bit of gossip. Then. "Did you hear the news about Tezza?" she finally asked.

Oh no! I thought with a sinking feeling, *He's done it. He must have decided to bring the date forward.* "What news?"

"Tezza's dead!" The news was such a shock that nothing registered, just numbness.

"How did that happen?" I waited, expecting to hear that the doctored car had blown up, or that there had been a revenge killing exacted after many years. I doubted his cancer got him that soon!

"Well, you know he goes to the club every Sunday and gets the courtesy bus home? Yesterday he had a few more than usual. He was legless. Told the staff he was celebrating a special occasion that was planned for this week. The bus pulled up in front of his house, he wobbled off, missed the kerb, stumbled, and hit his head on a rock. He's dead!"

I had mixed feelings. Primarily I was sorry that he had gone that way, but maybe it was a better way, seeing that he had cancer? I felt extreme relief. I didn't have to dob in a mate, but I knew that

I would have had to do it. This fortuitous event meant that the Aussie code didn't have to be broken.

The day of the funeral arrived. Tezza had a big funeral at Palmdale. He had plenty of mates that he'd gathered on his drinking circuit. He had some mates still alive from the old days too, the ones who knew when to quit. Many had settled on the Central Coast in the '80s, particularly around Ettalong, Umina and Booker Bay. So they celebrated and reminisced at the Woy Woy Club. Tezza is buried near his deceased mates in the Point Clare Cemetery.

Tezza, you had a big heart for a little bloke and were always willing to help out a mate: a heart like Phar Lap—and a champion like him to boot!

The Rose

There is a special person who must be mentioned: a woman with a heart as big as the Broadwater. A woman who welcomed all into the pub and looked after them and the pub as if it were her own home: Junie MacDonald, aka The Rose.

Junie Mac was a truly amazing woman. I will always remember her for her rendition of *The Rose* by Bette Midler. Junie sang it whenever requested, and on karaoke nights, the whole hotel stopped and silence lingered for a while after she had finished. Then, of course, the hubbub started again, but for a while Junie had held us in her hands.

"You'll be late for your own funeral, June," lamented Junie's husband, Kenny Mac the truck driver, one night, as he rolled his eyes, nodded his head and lifted his bulk off the bar stool, whilst at the same time draining the last drops from his schooner. Kenny was ready to go home.

"Come on, Junie," he'd shout, shaking his head again. "Come on woman. Can't yer stop talkin'?"

Kenny was 190cm tall and weighed 125kg. Junie was 152cm and weighed 55kg. Junie was never fazed by Kenny. She always finished her current conversation and had at least four more conversations before she got to the public bar door. And if she saw a few schooner glasses on the way that needed picking up, well, she'd do that too!

We left Kincumber in 2006. Junie became ill with cirrhosis of the liver, and died not long after on 4 June 2007. I was overseas at the time, but I did hear the story of her funeral and I think you should hear it too! As expected, there was a big turnout.

Not only was Junie much-loved at the hotel, she was a tireless worker for the local football team and for the community as a whole. She organised raffles at the footy grounds, helped at community and sporting barbeques, and at charity events, and managed to fit in calling the meat raffles at the pub on a Friday night. Mind you, she needed a few schooners to go the distance, but could always be counted upon! She knew everybody and everything that happened. At times she had had a hard life, but it only seemed to temper her heart of gold.

Junie's memorial service was to take place at the Sculpture Gardens at Kincumber. There is a lovely chapel there set amongst the trees, sculptures and flowers. And it was only a short drive to the pub for a wake—an added advantage!

Came the day and everything was ready for Junie's last solo: flowers, people, music and tears… Junie didn't turn up.

Junie was waiting at Palmdale Funeral Home at Ourimbah, about 20 kilometres away. It had been raining heavily for days before the funeral and the roads were flooded. So she didn't get to Kincumber.

"You'll be late for your own funeral," Kenny had said. She was.

Rest in Peace, Junie. As long as *The Rose* is sung, you will never be forgotten.

There are characters in every pub. There are characters in all walks of life. But the microcosm that is a pub distils them into one brew. Kincumber was one such brew, but equally importantly, it was the most community-minded pub I have ever owned. I doubt that there are many such mixtures elsewhere in Australia.

The Meeting Place

There are meeting places in all cultures and the Kincumber had been a meeting place for many thousands of years before the white man arrived with his bibles and his culture. The hotel was located on the Broadwater and at the base of the Kincumber Mountain. Kincumba is an Aboriginal word meaning "towards the rising sun". It was an important cultural site for the Guringai (many spellings) people who were the traditional owners of the land stretching from the Hawkesbury to Norah Head. But like the bars on a Friday night when discussions got heated, there was disagreement about this, and the answer depended upon to whom you were speaking. The Darkinyung (also many spellings) mob claimed that they were custodians of the Guringai land. The hotel had been built many years previously when indigenous culture and land was largely disregarded and many of the traditional owners were killed or scattered. It was built on what archaeologists term "disturbed land", as it had been thoroughly disturbed by agriculture, grazing and buildings.

But the retirement village around the hotel was not so disturbed. It was built on the Broadwater site, where there were still the remains of middens, a Bora ring, and carved trees. Again, details vary depending upon to whom you speak. To some, this land brought an ancient peace; to others who disturbed this site, it brought unrest. So this too paralleled the life that swirled within the hotel's walls. Inside the hotel, there was a calmness and respect now that had been brought out of earlier unrest within. The hotel had settled into its reputation as a safe place. It was a welcome place for indigenous as well white people. Kamilaroi and Wiradjuri people came to have a drink and a yarn with the Kincumber Devil, as I was known, because I had agitated hard, but fruitlessly, to save the surrounding site.

The local nickname for the Kincumber Hotel was the "Cucumber" and it was full of great characters, many of whom were related. A big family. It was probably no accident that the physical layout of the pub—two long, parallel, bungalow-type buildings connected by a courtyard—resembled a meeting place. Patrons lived their lives interconnected like threads, the physical parallel of which was the toing and froing across the courtyard as they moved from bar to bistro. Equally, with respect, they could be called the Kincumber mob. Of the diverse and many characters who drank there when I arrived, many deserve a mention, but I'll settle for a few.

There was Swanny the Concreter. He couldn't be mistaken as anything other than a concreter. He was the ultimate walking, self-advertising tradie: blue King Gee shorts, Blundstone boots, wearing his "Ken Swan Concreting" pale-blue T-shirt. Mind you, a great many Kincumber locals wore those T-shirts. The name Ken Swan was known far and wide. A great, big-hearted man. He *was* big, too—not tall but well-upholstered; happy face; schooner of Toohey's New in hand; a man who regarded the pub as his lounge room and all who walked into it as his guests. His eagle eye never missed the hesitant newcomer stepping into the smoky, happily humming public bar.

"How are you mate? Looking for someone?"

"Yeah. Ian (aka the Philosopher)."

"He's over there at the end of the bar, mate. I'll take you across."

In comes another likely lad.

"How are you, mate? Been here before? No? Let me buy you a beer. What are you having?"

So Swanny would chat him up, find out all his business and tell him all the pub's. Fair exchange. He didn't leave them until they felt at home and had been introduced to a few other regulars. Swanny knew everyone, liked everyone, and was liked by all. There was another side to Swanny, a part of his nature that accounted for his popularity. As well as helping anyone, he helped many sporting bodies. He and some mates, including Trev of "Mustang Sally" fame, would cut into valuable drinking time on a Friday or Saturday afternoon to run the raffle for the Fisho's club or to man the free barbie on special occasions such as Anzac Day, or to sizzle for the football club, Kate's Rugby Union team, or for a charity event. Then there was the gentle Swanny. The family man. Swanny has two daughters, Chantelle and Kirsten. When little, they would sit in the beer garden with their chips and soft drink, as did the other kids. They were as well known and liked as their father.

Just as there is a link between pub buildings and between two cultures, there is a link between Swanny and another well-loved character—Mick Garrett. The link is Jenny: a feisty, no-nonsense lady with a ready laugh and huge smile. Jenny is Mick's ex-wife and partner of Swanny. She keeps Swanny on the straight and narrow. To his credit and Jenny's, he no longer drinks but is still an important part of Kincumber pub life. As many of the customers are related through bonds of friendship and family, the first rule of the Kincumber is "Don't say anything about anyone" because in nine cases out of ten, you are talking to that someone's aunt, uncle, cousin or mother. So you would be with Swanny, Jenny, Mick and Lorraine. Enough philosophy and sentimentality. On to Mick.

Mick was a leprechaun. A leprechaun who looked up at you with big brown eyes in a perpetually tanned face, his head held to the left, his voice a distinctive type of slow drawl.

"How are you this morning, Lllllllynette?" he would unfailingly intone. Dry voice. Dry sense of humour. Somehow the morning always felt brighter when he was there to greet you, duller when he was not.

Mick came into his own identity with his carpet cleaning business. No self-promoting blue T-shirt for him. A blue singlet was fine as his uniform, worn winter and summer with regulation shorts and runners. We were lucky the day we contracted Mick as the hotel cleaner. But Mick was lucky the day Lorraine became his partner, both personally and professionally. She kept him hard at work and that was a tough job in itself. Lorraine was taller than

283

Mick, with brown hair, brown eyes and a voice that brooks no nonsense. She and Mick were a match made in heaven. She'd go her way, follow her routine (you could set the bar clock by her arrival and departure times), and matched Mick drink for drink— one middy of beer for Lorraine, one bourbon and Coke for Mick—preferably sitting at their favourite table near the door. Their routine was so inflexible that they followed it on their twice-yearly trips to Bali. They stayed at the same hotel at Kuta, drank at the same bar (naturally same time, same table), and only partook of the same snacks they ate in Australia: chips, and cheese and biscuits brought from Australia in two suitcases.

Both Lorraine and Mick had been cleaning the hotel for a few years when we sold it. I had a morning routine of walking around the hotel's external and internal areas, checking the cleaning and that any directives I may have given the day before were done. I was notorious for the notes I would leave the staff. "The taps in the washbasins—ladies' toilet, saloon bar—aren't clean enough. Use a toothbrush to clean around the bases. Thanks, Lyn." I always said "Thank you"!

I walked into the pub at about 6 p.m., 18 months after selling it, and one of the first people I met was Lorraine. She had had a few schooners—what hardworking cleaner doesn't?—and the first thing she said to me was, "I didn't think I would ever miss your little love notes, but I do."

Ain't love strange?

I revisited the pub again for a very sad occasion—Mick's funeral, one of the biggest I have seen. Tribute was paid to two things: the esteem in which he was held in the community, and his fighting spirit. Mick died of aggressive lung cancer on 15 April, three days short of his 58th birthday, a date he was hoping to keep.

No pub story would be complete without mention of a few customers. The bottom end of the public bar was "home" to a few of the punters. One of these was Kenny Fraser, brother to Dawn and a landmark in the bar. He was a funny fellow, had his ways, and his most important job was to hold the meat raffle tickets and check the numbers for all of the girls on a Friday night. Not a problem for him! Kenny did love the girls! Mind you, he was lucky himself and often went home with a few meat trays.

The top end of the public bar was a little different. When we arrived it was home to a large crew, many of whom are no longer with us. For a while it was dubbed "God's Waiting Room" in jest by the regulars, as it began to thin of patrons. At that end of the bar there was a skylight and one wag used to often say, "Beam them up, Scotty!" Scotty got a bit too active and instead the guys took on their own active duty on terra firma. They became custodians of the public bar library, many volumes in a glass-fronted bookcase—a duty they took seriously (there wasn't a library in Kincumber at that time). There seemed to be a propensity of Zane Grey novels in the bookcase! The rules were that you left a book, you borrowed a book. Bad luck if you weren't liked: you didn't get to first base. The keeper of the keys conveniently "lost" them when that patron was in. The library was only open in the mornings, when the guys could check the books in and out.

We now move into the saloon bar, home of the racing crowd:

punters, owners, breeders and trainers. The tips that flew around were phenomenal! Billy the Dog Man was one such trainer and legend. I remember one Christmas when Billy and his wife, Narelle, brought me in a big box of Darrell Lea chocolates. I loved them. Unfortunately, so did Brian the Publican. He was ecstatic when I received my present—you would have sworn they were his!

"Don't worry, Booma," said Bill the Dog Man, "I've got a better present for you, but I haven't got it with me. You'll get it next week." Brian the Publican's eyes lit up: he envisaged an enormous box of Darrell Lea!

Next week came. In came Bill, as happy and excited as a dog man could be.

"You have to come to my house, Booma, to get your present."

Up we went. Bill had a great training facility for his greyhounds, set up in his garage. He proudly opened the door and there was a great-looking dog.

"Isn't it something, Booma? Narelle and I have given you a share in Magic Toll as your Christmas present." Brian the Publican's mouth dropped. The Darrell Lea light went out in his eyes.

"Thanks," he managed to say.

Nevertheless, Bill, the saloon bar guys, Kevin Munford and Swanny had lots of fun at the Gosford and Wyong dogs with Magic Toll. It was always going to win and did once. Great excitement, but it blotted its copybook. Horrors! Magic Toll stopped in the middle of the track and bit another dog. Three times and you're out was the ruling. Magic Toll was soon out.

There is another dog story of a different kind. Bob Martin, another public bar stalwart, had a wicked sense of humour and outdid himself one day with his particular "dog trick". An ad had appeared on television showing a guy sitting at the bar of a pub with his dog sitting beside him. In the ad, the publican told the man to leave, as under the *Health Act*, dogs are not allowed on licensed premises, with the exception of guide dogs. With great affront, the man said of the mutt that was with him, "He's a guide dog, mate!" "Out!" pointed the publican.

One Friday night, the punting crowd was sitting around in the saloon bar, busy with their schooners, happily discussing with great authority anything that ran on four legs. Into the public bar came Bob Martin. There was stunned silence and then a great roar of laughter, heralded by Shaz in the Public Bar. All heads turned! Bob was slowly feeling his way into the saloon bar, white stick tapping the ground in front of him, sunglasses on—and a chihuahua on a lead beside him.

These are only a few of the characters and yarns that made this a unique pub. There was always something happening. Usually it was funny. Sometimes it was dramatic. Kincumber had its own personality and its own rich cultural history, from indigenous to white. This was reflected in the easy mixing of customers. It stood apart from our other pubs with its mix of tolerant, caring people.

The Last Hurrah

We had been ten years at Kincumber, had fought lots of battles, and thought that it was time to sell. It was a great pub, with the best of locals and drinkers, but for some reason we seemed to have a clock built into our working lives that said "Ten years up: time to move on". There were family reasons as well. My daughter Kate, extremely capable, wanted to become more independent and try something on her own. Brian the Publican had his own plans. We had been going more and more frequently to Singapore to visit my friend Bernice, who had just started working and living there.

"Bernice will be lonely and needs some friends to visit her," Brian kept repeating.

All this was reasonable and we visited once, then twice, a year. Then it became four times a year.

"Brian, it's not necessary to go across so often. Bernice has settled in and has lots of friends."

"I'll go by myself if you don't want to come."

So we both went. Bernice and I didn't realise that Brian enjoyed the Singapore life so much. Sure, he went out with the boys—Tom, Grainger and Bertie—and we thought he just liked to be out and have a drink. It turned out to be more than that. Brian liked meeting the Singapore girls. He liked the lifestyle. So his underlying reason for selling was to get back to Singapore and start a bar/bistro there. I had no clue. And no reason to sell except the ten-year clock.

The hotel went on the market. The publicans who knew Brian and looked over it did not buy. They knew we were good operators and they feared the hotel was at its peak. But the size of the property and the potential of the land around it attracted a unique man, Tom Hedley. Tom was a great bloke who combined his love of the pub life with his occupation as a developer. Tom started his working life in Queensland, and as a young tradesman he used to go into the pub at lunchtime to have two schooners and two pies.

"One day, Brian, I was standing there and I thought, why am I paying for two schooners each day when I could own the pub and other people could be standing here buying my beer."

So Tom bought his first pub and liked the idea so much that he bought many more, mostly in NSW and Queensland, and ours was one of the first of these. We had the bottle shop over in Kincumber Village Shopping Centre, the drive-in bottle shop at the pub, plus the large pub itself, which had potential for further development. But the drawcard was the land around it. Tom had his building company with a team of architects and a management team behind him, so it suited him. He did up the bottle shop and the hotel, but when he had no luck with the council passing the plans he had for the other areas, Tom sold.

I have many fond memories of my time at Kincumber, of the hotel patrons and of the community at large. They were a real community and they supported us and we supported them. In our years, the pub really was the hub of the community. We sponsored sporting bodies, raised money for them, raised money for many charities, Father Chris O'Reilly's being one. If a family was in financial trouble and needed money for medical care, the hotel was open to them for fundraising. We made the hotel a safe place for the families and myriad retirees who lived in the area. Older patrons came there as kids, drank there as adults, celebrated milestones in their lives there, and were farewelled there for their wake.

All I can wish the residents of Kincumber, and the present patrons, is health and happiness. You made us part of your community. You made my bar your lounge room . Thank you.

Kincumber was to be my last pub. Brian the Publican and I divorced in 2011 and since then, I continue to live a full and happy life—travelling, writing and spending time with friends, family members and grandchildren.

EPILOGUE

The era I have written about is gone. The family-owned pub is now the company-owned pub. There were some characteristics of this era that can never be replicated.

The most telling one is probably "Let's go down to the pub. I know the publican. He's a good bloke". The "good bloke" welcomed you into his lounge room, a cosy place with carpet on the floor and upholstered chairs. Nothing sterile or noisy. We wanted you to stay.

This was an era before computers. A paper and list era. There were lists of things to be done, cleaning lists, daily supervisory lists. There were pages of reconciliations and stocktakes. There was no computer to list stock on hand, stock to be reordered, or to do the weekly wages.

The computer is only as good as the operator, and human nature never changes. I don't know if I ran my pubs with tough love, but I do know I looked after my staff and they in turn looked after me, the customers and the pub. We all took pride in our workplace.

It was a hard life, but always a rewarding and fun one. I wouldn't change a thing.

ACKNOWLEDGEMENTS

In the years between writing this book and leaving it languishing in a drawer, I have been encouraged by the support of many.

A huge thank you to Jan Cornall, my editor, mentor and friend, who first heard my stories and believed that I could write a book that would be enjoyed by many, and would provide enough laughs to be an escape from a sometimes depressing world.

Many, many thanks to David M. Moore, a patron and friend from the Union days. He simply told me to "get on with it" and, when my confidence was lowest, introduced me to characters who lived through this era and who, in turn, encouraged me to take it out of the drawer and keep going.

To long-suffering Jacqui Buswell, Anna Yang, Margie Yen and Di Godbier. Thanks, girls, for your listening and story reading. I seemed to be so needy at times and you always rallied to the call. To Caroline Jones whose comments never failed to keep me writing. And a special thanks to Carmen Dingwall and to Sally Asnicar for their detailed proofing, correcting and layout, and to Christine Scott for painstakingly reading the finished proof. Thank you, Debbie Hambly, for your patience and encouragement, and Kerryn McMillan for helping with last-minute changes.

A very special thank you to Margaret and Philip Luker for their unfailing support, encouragement and practical suggestions.

Thank you, family—Danielle, Kate and Brian. You lived and survived through this era, and have your own funny stories to tell. And to Brian the Publican—a larger than life character who added so much colour to these stories and to pub life.

To all my patrons in all the hotels, you made my life fun, exciting and always interesting. There would not be a book or memories without you.

CPSIA information can be obtained
at www.ICGtesting.com
Printed in the USA
BVHW040918130919
558387BV00016B/333/P